ST. AUGUSTINE

AGAINST THE ACADEMICS

CONTRA ACADEMICOS

Ancient Christian Writers

THE WORKS OF THE FATHERS IN TRANSLATION

EDITED BY

JOHANNES QUASTEN, S. T. D.
*Professor of Ancient Church History
and Christian Archaeology*

JOSEPH C. PLUMPE, Ph. D.
*Professor of Patristic Greek
and Ecclesiastical Latin*

The Catholic University of America
Washington, D. C.

No. 12

ST. AUGUSTINE

AGAINST THE ACADEMICS

TRANSLATED AND ANNOTATED

BY

JOHN J. O'MEARA

M. A., D. PHIL. (OXON)

*Professor of Latin at University College
Dublin, Ireland*

NEWMAN PRESS

New York, N.Y./Ramsey, N.J.

Nihil Obstat:

Johannes Quasten, S.T.D.
Censor Deputatus

Imprimatur:

Patricius A. O'Boyle, D.D.
Archiepiscopus Washingtonensis
15 December 1950

Library of Congress
Catalog Card Number: 78-62461

ISBN: 0-8091-0252-8

PUBLISHED BY PAULIST PRESS
Editorial Office: 1865 Broadway, New York, N.Y. 10023
Business Office: 545 Island Road, Ramsey, N.J. 07446

PRINTED AND BOUND IN THE UNITED STATES OF AMERICA

CONTENTS

ST. AUGUSTINE

AGAINST THE ACADEMICS

Augustine, *Retractationes* 1. 1. 1, 4: When, therefore, I had abandoned both what I had achieved of the ambitions of this world and what I wished to achieve, and had betaken myself to the peace and calm of the Christian life, and before I was baptized, I wrote first the *Against the Academics* or *On the Academics*. I purposed by the most cogent reasoning I could muster to rid my mind of the arguments of the Academics. For they cause many to despair of finding truth and prevent the wise man from assenting to anything or granting anything at all as clear and manifest, since to them everything appears obscure and uncertain. These arguments were troubling me also. Through the Lord's mercy and help I succeeded in my design. . . .

This work begins thus: "*O utinam, Romaniane, hominem sibi aptum.*"

INTRODUCTION

1

THE DIALOGUES OF CASSICIACUM

The *Contra Academicos* (three books), *De beata vita,* and *De ordine* (two books) form a series of dialogues which may be called the *Dialogues of Cassiciacum.* They are the earliest extant works of St. Augustine, and purport to be the touched-up records of actual disputations held by Augustine and his friends at Cassiciacum (near Milan) during the month of November A. D. 386. Shortly before this time Augustine had undergone a mental and moral crisis during which his physical health had been impaired. Shortly after, he retired to Milan to be baptized. These dialogues claim to give a reliable picture of the mind and way of life of one of the greatest figures of the West, precisely at the moment which was for him most critical and vital. They are inextricably bound up with one another: they were not written in order, but one book of one work was followed by one book of another, and so on.[1] According to the more usually received sequence, *Contra Academicos 1* opened the series, and *Contra Academicos 3* was the last but one in the group. Closely associated with these dialogues are the *Soliloquia,* which were, at least in part, written simultaneously with the whole series, and the early *Epistolae* of Augustine to his absent friends.

2

THE INTERLOCUTORS

A. *Augustine*

The life of Augustine is too well known for us to give anything but the merest outline of his career up to the date of his baptism in 387. There is, however, one aspect of his earlier life which must be stressed if we are to understand the full significance of his conversion, and appreciate the psychological attitude that was his when he wrote the work with which we are concerned. It is an aspect which is usually lost sight of because of the absorbing interest of the story of his moral and intellectual experiences before this date. We refer to the question of his worldly ambitions and success. As we look back through the ages to the scene of his wrestling with God, we tend to forget that Augustine's problems were made much more difficult by the very human preoccupation of work to be done and a living to be made, not only for himself, but for those that depended on him. At the time of his conversion he had the prize of success well within his grasp. Was he to surrender all, jeopardize all, for an idea that only with difficulty convinced him? It was from his own experience of Grace at this juncture that he became its ardent apostle.

Augustine (Aurelius Augustinus) was born at Tagaste in Numidia in November, 354, of a heathen father, Patricius, and a Christian mother, Monnica.[2] After some schooling in his native town, he was sent to a teacher in the neighbouring city of Madauros, for Patricius had already seen that the boy showed great promise, and had determined that no chance would be denied his son. That son was later to censure his parents for their too great interest in a worldly career for him: "for they were regardless how I should employ what they forced me to learn, except to satiate the insatiate desires of a wealthy beggary and a shameful glory." [3] Nevertheless, the boy responded to the encouragement given by his parents, and soon earned the compliment of being acclaimed above his fellow scholars for his excellence in declamation.[4]

His preliminary studies completed, he spent his sixteenth year at home in Tagaste—idle. His father meanwhile got together the means to send him to Carthage, there to take up studies to become a professional rhetorician: "Who did not extol my father, for that beyond the ability of his means, he would furnish his son with all necessaries for a far journey for his studies' sake? . . . But while in that my sixteenth year I lived with my parents, leaving all school for a while, . . . the briers of unclean desires grew rank over my head, and there was no hand to root them out." [5] Even his mother was so keen for his worldly success that she, too, was negligent about the fate of his soul.[6]

On his arrival in Carthage, Augustine immediately proceeded to win distinction: "And now I was chief in the rhetoric school, whereat I joyed proudly, and I swelled with arrogancy." [7] Ambition began to stir in the heart of the young man himself. He hoped, doubtless, to arrive at the highest grade of his profession, if not actually the highest of the imperial civil service. All his hopes, however, were suddenly threatened by the death of his father.

It was only with the greatest difficulty, and aided, probably, by Romanianus, a wealthy magnate of his native town, that his mother managed to keep him on at Carthage.

When he was nineteen years of age, he came upon the *Hortensius* of Cicero.[8] The book made a profound and lasting impression on him. From it he conceived a passion for truth, which, at the time, he believed was to be found in the Sacred Scriptures. When, however, he opened the sacred book he felt disappointed. He cast about for some guide to truth and fell under the influence of the Manichees, who professed to lead men to truth merely by the light of reason and without employing any authority.[9] For almost a decade Augustine was not only a Manichee, but an ardent apostle of Manicheism. The full import of this fact upon his mind and later development was enormous.[10]

When he had finished his studies, he returned to Tagaste, a Manichee, "swelling with pride." Monnica refused to receive him into her house, but his friend and patron, Romanianus,[11] was only too willing to help the young man.[12] Moreover, he paid him the compliment of following him into Manicheism, and entrusted to him the education of his son, Licentius. Soon, however, Augustine saw an opportunity of becoming a professional rhetorician at Carthage, whither he returned after a year's absence. In his *Confessions* he gives a good picture of the bustle and anxiety of his life at this period: "For this space of nine years . . . we lived seduced and seducing, deceived and deceiving, in divers lusts; openly, by sciences which they call liberal; secretly, with a false-named religion; here proud, there superstitious, everywhere vain. Here hunting after the emptiness of popular praise, down even to theatrical applauses, and poetic prizes, and strifes for grassy garlands, and the follies of shows, and the intemperance of desires. . . . In those years I taught rhetoric, and, overcome by cupidity, made sale of a loquacity to overcome by." [18] In his anxiety he began to take a deep interest in the occult dealings of divination.[14] At this time, too, he wrote his first book: *De pulchro et apto*, which is, unfortunately, no longer extant. It dealt with the general problem of aesthetics, and seems to have been a bid for recognition by Rome. At any rate, it was dedicated to a certain Hierius, a Syrian, who had made good at Rome, and Augustine was soon on his way to the heart of the Empire. He hoped to emulate the Syrian.

About the time of the composition of the *De pulchro et apto* he seems to have read a good deal of philosophy— enough, at any rate, to give a philosophical flavour to this first work of his.[15] He began also to see that the Manichean cosmology was childish in comparison with that of the professional philosophers. His doubts about Manicheism were transformed into profound dissatisfaction as a result of an interview with a certain Faustus, who, he had been assured, was to set his mind at ease. He naturally gravitated towards the scepticism of the New Academy.[16] This at once encouraged him to concentrate upon material success, and left him disturbed in the depths of his being.

In the autumn of 383 Augustine set out for Rome. He denies that he went there solely to make more money, or gain greater distinction in his profession. His friends had assured him that these things were, indeed, to be had at Rome, and he admits that these considerations had some weight with him. His primary reason, he says, was that he had been led to expect that the pupils there would be better behaved than they were at Carthage. In this he was to be disappointed,[17] although through his pupils he soon began to be known.[18] About a year after his arrival in the city he was appointed, through the influence of the urban prefect, Symmachus, to be master of rhetoric at Milan, then the seat of the imperial court.[19]

At this point we would do well to consider the *milieu* in which Augustine lived and worked, and what his chances of high preferment were.

Hierius was not the only provincial who had gained considerable success in coming to Rome and Milan. Ausonius, for example, from being a teacher for thirty years at Bordeaux, became tutor of Gratian and thereby helped himself and his family to all the principal magistracies of the West.[20] Neoterius, who started life as a simple clerk, was taken up by Symmachus, and became prefect and eventually consul. Palladius, who came to Rome five years ahead of Augustine, became, on Symmachus' recommendation, master of the offices. Symmachus helped Pacatus, who came to Rome six years later than Augustine and recited a panegyric before Theodosius, to be made proconsul of Africa in 390. Others, including Priscianus, Marinianus, and Theodorus, were helped by Symmachus, about the time when Augustine was appointed to his position in Milan, to the acquisition of very high offices.[21]

The career of the last-mentioned, Flavius Manlius (Mallius) Theodorus,[22] is of particular interest, because he was a friend of Augustine and, as we can gather from various indications, must have had considerable influence upon him.[23] This man, to whom Augustine addressed the *De beata vita,* and to whose works he refers in the *De ordine* [24] (both works contemporary with the *Contra Academicos*) as models which he himself could follow in his dialogues, was born,[25] about the same time as Augustine, of poor parents, as it would seem, in Milan. He passed in the usual way through the rhetorical schools and legal profession into the imperial civil service. He then retired to Liguria to write philosophical dialogues,[26] but was soon recalled to public service. He was consul in 399.[27]

Augustine might, then, hope for high preferment indeed. He found himself at Milan in a conspicuous position close to the emperor and his court. Before a year had elapsed, he had delivered a panegyric on the occasion of the consulship (385) of Bauto,[28] who held all power during the minority of Valentinian. Such distinction could, as we have seen, lead to the fulfilment of the highest ambitions. It is clear that Augustine was at this time consumed with anxiety over success, and overworked both in his profession and in canvassing powerful friends.[29] The tempo of his life increased to straining point: "I panted after honours, gains, marriage, . . . and my heart was panting with these anxieties, and boiling with the feverishness of consuming thoughts." [30]

But other factors had begun to enter his life—to add, however, only more immediate confusion and turmoil in his soul. His moral and intellectual experiences were exacting indeed. From Ambrose he expected much help, but got little, if any, of that personal direction for which his soul yearned.[31] Even while he pursued worldly ambitions, he began to think of abandoning them for a life devoted to the service of God. And yet he paused: "We must not lightly abandon them, for it were a shame to return again to them. See, it is no great matter now to obtain some station, and then what should we more wish for? We have a store of powerful friends; if nothing else offer, and we be in much haste, at least a presidentship may be given us. . . ." [32]

Let us take up very briefly the story of his moral and intellectual difficulties. His mother, although a good Christian, was but a woman of her day when she had wished to postpone the sacrament of baptism for Augustine until the surge of adolescence had passed. It is not surprising that Augustine, in the times and circumstances in which he lived, did not altogether resist the allurements of the flesh, and that neither the *Hortensius* nor Manicheism had any practical influence on his behaviour.

More serious were his difficulties about God's nature,[33] the problem of evil in the world, and the Scriptures. In these questions Manicheism was to prove a positive hindrance. Eventually, he understood that the Catholic Church did not teach what he had been led to believe that it taught; in fact, Ambrose could make it appear that the Catholic teaching was defensible.[34]

Many circumstances and considerations led him little by little to seek for baptism: his mother's dreams of his conversion, in which, at that time, he put great credit; the fear of death, which seems to have affected him in his weakened state of health;[35] the Platonist books,[36] which opened up for him vistas of spiritual reality till then undreamt of; the reading of St. Paul and the Scriptures; the story of the conversion of a fellow countryman, rhetorician, and Platonist—Victorinus;[37] the importunate example of the monks of Egypt as presented to him by

Pontitianus; and finally, the dramatic crisis in the garden from which Augustine represents himself emerging as an earnest "convert."

Shortly after this crisis Augustine, in the autumn of 386, resigned his office—and with it all hope of worldly success—on the plea of impaired health, and retired to Cassiciacum, a country villa belonging to a friend, Verecundus, at some distance from Milan. There with his mother, Alypius, Licentius, Trygetius, and a few others, he adopted a mode of life which is sufficiently well reflected in the *Contra Academicos* and the other *Dialogues of Cassiciacum*. A few months later, early in 387, he was baptized in Milan. Although he recovered his health, he never returned to the career which had meant so much for him. An all-absorbing interest had entered his life. In his early writings, the *Dialogues,* we are privileged to see his mind adjusting itself to its new aspirations. It would be surprising indeed, if we see there no trace of his former thoughts also. We shall see, too, some of the splendour of the vision that enchanted him.

B. *Alypius*

Alypius [38] was a native of Tagaste where his parents were among the most distinguished people of the municipality. He was a blood-relation of Romanianus, the friend and patron of Augustine. He studied under the latter at Tagaste and Carthage, preceded him to Rome, accompanied him to Milan and Cassiciacum, and with him was baptized. He was marked out by his parents for a career at the bar, and in his professional duties showed integrity and courage. He was devoted to Augustine, sharing all his confidences, and, while showing much independence of mind, was, nevertheless, greatly influenced—to becoming a Manichee, for instance—by his master. He had great nobility of character, led a strict life, and was honest and vigorous in all things. Soon after his baptism he returned to Africa with Augustine, there shortly to become bishop of his native town, Tagaste.

C. *Licentius*

Licentius [39] was the son of Romanianus and was educated by Augustine, who always took a great interest in his welfare. He followed Augustine to Carthage, and is found again with him in Cassiciacum, where he was about to begin a study of philosophy. He is represented as being then very young. [40] He was something of a poet, unstable, impulsive, and ambitious. He caused untold anxiety to his father, to Augustine, and to all his friends. He gave up philosophy—if indeed he ever had any interest in it—and seems to have been remiss also in the practice of his religion. His one ambition was to be consul. R. Lanciani [41] says that his body was discovered in St. Lorenzo in Rome in 1862, and that there was evidence to prove that he had attained senatorial rank, and had died a Christian.

D. *Trygetius*

The sum total of our information on this interlocutor is taken from the *Dialogues of Cassiciacum* themselves. We are told that he was a fellow citizen and pupil of

Augustine; that he was fond of history; and that he had
been in military service, which he had preferred to the
tedium of learning. In the *Dialogues*, however, he is
represented as being then most eager for knowledge and
still very young.[42]

E. *Navigius*

Of this brother of Augustine we know very little. We
first hear of him as being with Augustine in Cassiciacum.
That he was a real brother appears from the *Confessions*,[43]
where he is shown to have been present at the death of his
mother Monnica. He may have been the father of Augustine's nephew, Patricius.[44]

F. *Romanianus*

Most of our information about Romanianus comes from
the prefaces to the first and second books of the *Contra
Academicos*. It has been suggested that he was a relative
of Augustine.[45] The latter, however, in his many references to him never once makes mention of any relationship whatever. Moreover, Augustine, in recounting Romanianus' claims upon himself, would hardly fail to in-
clude such an obvious tie as relationship.[46] Finally,
Paulinus of Nola, who was not likely to have been ignorant
on such a point, seems deliberately to exclude all such
connection.[47]

He was one of the principal citizens of Tagaste, and
was both wealthy and generous. We have already seen
something of the help he gave to, and the interest he took
in, Augustine. He came to Milan, while the latter was

there, to plead at the imperial court in connection with some domestic lawsuit in which his wealth was involved.[48] The *Contra Academicos,* which was addressed to him, was meant—among other things—to lead Romanianus to take a more serious interest in philosophy and to have greater confidence in it.[49] It had a companion volume, the *De vera religione,* which was projected at the time of the *Contra Academicos* and was sent to Romanianus a few years later. It sought to convince him that the Christian faith was the true religion.[50] Romanianus did become a Christian, and ever remained a faithful friend and follower of Augustine.[51] The name Romanianus is found in conjunction with the gentile name "Cornelius" on an inscription from Tagaste.[52]

3

THE *CONTRA ACADEMICOS* AND THE *ACADEMICA* OF CICERO

There is no doubt but that Cicero's *Academica* was the primary source upon which Augustine drew both for his version of the teaching of the New Academy, and also, in part, for his refutation of the same.

Clear acknowledgement is made in the *Contra Academicos* of its dependence upon the *Academica.* Thus, for example, when Augustine undertakes to give a more detailed refutation of the New Academy, he is particularly anxious to justify his defection from Cicero's authority.[53] Licentius is recommended to read the *Academica.*[54] There are many instances of reference to, and quotation from, it.[55] The correspondence in language between the two works has been noted.[56] But indeed the very title of Augustine's work; the dialogue form in which it is cast; the fact that very little matter is brought forward by Augustine which was not already found in Cicero—all make demonstration of this point superfluous.[57]

A word must here be said about the New Academy. It received its name because of its relations with the "Old" Academy, that is to say, the Academy founded by Plato. From this Academy it had sprung, but, as the name implies, it had also marked itself off from the original body. The Old Academy was the Academy of Plato, his pupils, and their successors from the time of its foundation in Athens about 385 B. C. until the time of Arcesilas (ca. 315-241/40 B. C.).[58] In general, its doctrine was positive. Although it placed no confidence whatever in the perceptions of the senses, it did put absolute trust in intellectual cognition. Arcesilas, in denying the possibility of any knowledge, gave the Academy, over which he presided at the time, a sceptical turn, and, accordingly, was considered to have founded a "New," "Second," or "Middle" Academy. Carneades (214/213-129/128 B. C.),[59] in systematizing the negative criticism of the Middle Academy and developing a technique whereby he was enabled to argue convincingly for both sides of any problem, was considered to have advanced the Academy even more upon the road of scepticism, and was, therefore, regarded as the founder of the "Third" or "New" Academy. Cicero at times professed that he was a follower of the New Academy, and his *Academica* was written as an outline and defence of their position. The influence of the New Academy persisted spasmodically until the fifth century

A. D. One should add that there were occasional attempts
made within the New Academy to return to the teaching
of the Old. The most notable of these was that of
Antiochus (130/120-68 B. C.).[60]

It will be remembered that Augustine, two or at most
three years before the date of the *Contra Academicos*
gave allegiance to the New Academy.[61] One of his first
steps, then, when he accepted the positive teaching of
Christ, was to refute the arguments of the New Academy.
The *Contra Academicos* is the result; and the spokesman
of the New Academy whom he challenges is Cicero in
his *Academica*.

The title of this work of Augustine's has assumed
varying forms. Now it appears as *"Contra Academicos"*; [62]
again as *"De Academicis"*; [63] and yet in other places as
simply *"Academicorum liber (libri)."* [64] The variation
finds justification in Augustine's own rather complex
attitude to the Academy (as we shall call the "New"
Academy from now on). This attitude reflects itself in
such phrases as: "I wrote *against* the Academics or *concerning* the Academics . . ."; [65] or, "I should never even by
way of joking attempt to attack the Academics. . . . I have
imitated rather than refuted them." [66] In short, the work
is both in opposition to, and in support of, the Academics.
Obviously, Augustine had no simple view of the Academy.
He believed, in fact, that it spoke with *two* voices.

Augustine gives an outline of the Academic position
in the following series of propositions: (1) Man can be
wise.[67] (2) That percept only can be comprehended
which manifests itself by signs that cannot belong to
what is not true.[68] (3) The Academic teaching is limited
to matters within the range of philosophical enquiry.[69]

(4) Since no such signs as are required by (2) are found, nothing can be perceived.[70] (5) As a result of (4), the wise man will never assent to anything.[71] (6) But since (5) logically leads to complete inaction, one must act according to what seems probable.[72] This is the position defended by Cicero in his *Academica,* and attacked by Augustine in the present work. Consequently, the book may with not a little justification be called *"Contra Academicos."* It will not be necessary to give here a summary of Augustine's arguments on this point: they are endlessly repeated in the course of the work, and are, it must be said, of little value.

But the Academic was also one, Augustine believed, who stood in the unbroken succession from Plato, and held the master's doctrine intact. For such a one he could have nothing but support: "I should never even by way of joking have attempted to attack the Academics. . . ." Hence, his work can be called *"De Academicis."* They had acted wisely in defending the masses from the sensationalism of the Stoics, by preaching that no knowledge whatever could be attained and by preserving for the few the spiritual message of Plato. But now men—even in the mass—had become capable of receiving all spiritual doctrine because of the cleansing and elevation of mankind through the coming of the Saviour. It was time for the Academy to cease from its negative and sceptical teaching. This is the real point of Augustine's book, and it is of the greatest interest and importance in our estimate of the sincerity of Augustine's spiritual conversion. The clear recognition of the Incarnation—a recognition based upon Augustine's own personal experience of the efficacy of the Grace that came to himself in the acceptance of the mystery, and which raised him so as to be able to follow ideals that had attracted but had proved impossible to him before then—is a compelling indication of his allegiance to Christ and His teaching. Unfortunately, although he appeals to Cicero as a witness, we have no good reason to believe that his theory about the Academy's second voice and a spiritual teaching has any foundation at all.[73]

4

THE IMPORTANCE OF THE
CONTRA ACADEMICOS

The *Contra Academicos* cannot be recommended as a valuable contribution to the theory of knowledge, nor even as an answer to scepticism. It is a personal work, written by Augustine to meet his own needs, and addressed to a friend of his. It is true that Augustine had some confidence in its arguments, and that the work was published; nevertheless, it bears too deeply the traces of experience to be in any sense an objective discussion of epistemology.

What is lost, however, could have been but of poor interest and importance in comparison with what is gained. In this work we have irrefutable evidence in connection with two important controversies dealing with Augustine, and the evidence is available precisely because the work is personal.

One of the controversies, debated for just over half a century, is still alive, and has received little notice in English. The other has arisen in a serious form only quite recently. What importance did Augustine in 386 attach to Neo-Platonism as compared with Christianity? That is the first question. The second is not unconnected. Who was, or were, the Neo-Platonist(s) whose writings admittedly played a striking part in his conversion?

A. *Augustine and Neo-Platonism* [74]

In 1888 appeared two contributions to Augustinian studies which, with commendable moderation, set the Augustine of the *Dialogues of Cassiciacum* over against the Augustine of the *Confessions;* the "philosopher" of Cassiciacum over against the Christian bishop of Hippo. Gaston Boissier [75] was content to explain the obvious element of truth in the contrast by supposing that Augustine changed his point of view. Adolf Harnack [76] went somewhat further in declaring that philosophy was Augustine's primary interest when he was at Cassiciacum, and that the *Confessions* really misrepresents his actual development; the *Dialogues,* he maintains, do not bear out the idea that Augustine was radically converted to Christianity.

Other scholars went much further. Loofs [77] came to the conclusion that even in 391, five years after his "conversion," Augustine was nothing more than a Neo-Platonist with a tincture of Christianity. Gourdon [78] maintained that the *Dialogues* and the *Confessions* represent two distinct "conversions" and show us "two different men": the *Dialogues* are in flagrant contradiction with the *Confessions;* [79] Augustine was entirely converted to Christianity only about 400.[80] Thimme [81] contended that the *Confes-*

sions were not to be trusted; that Augustine in 386 was neither a sincere Christian, nor free from Academic doubt; and that it was only gradually that he became first a complete Neo-Platonist and still later a Christian.

These views are well summed up and clearly stated in a work which is regarded with considerable respect by Augustinian scholars: Alfaric's *L'évolution intellectuelle de saint Augustin* I (Paris 1918). Lest we should seem to exaggerate the seriousness of the attack on the *Confessions,* we shall allow Alfaric to speak for himself:

(1) Quand il a reçu le baptême, il accordait si peu d'importance à ce rite que, dans les écrits de cette époque, où il parle fréquemment de lui-même et de tout ce qui l'intéresse, il n'y fait jamais la plus lointaine allusion. Il était alors assez peu catholique. Sans doute il acceptait la tradition chrétienne, mais il ne la considérait que comme une adaptation populaire de la sagesse platonicienne. Ce n'est que longtemps plus tard qu' il est arrivé à donner à la foi le pas sur la raison.[82]

(2) Moralement comme intellectuellement c'est au Néo-Platonisme qu' il s'est converti, plutôt qu' à l'Evangile.[83]

(3) Elle (Augustine's synthesis in 386) modifie assez sensiblement la doctrine du Maître (Plotinus) pour l'adapter aux enseignements de la foi catholique. Mais elle transforme encore davantage le Catholicisme pour le mettre d'accord avec la philosophie plotinienne et elle ne le considère que comme une forme inférieure de la sagesse, bonne seulement pour les intelligences faibles ou encore novices.[84]

(4) En lui le Chrétien disparaît derrière le disciple de Plotin. S' il était mort après avoir rédigé les *Soliloques,* . . . on ne le considérerait que comme un Néo-Platonicien convaincu, plus ou moins teinté de Christianisme.[85]

It is contended, then, that the *Confessions* mislead us: Augustine's baptism in 386 was not a serious affair—certainly not as serious as we are led to believe that it was; Augustine was first and foremost a Neo-Platonist. We are referred to the *Contra Academicos* and its companion dialogues for the proof of these assertions.[86]

Replies have been forthcoming to these charges. Among others, Wörter,[87] Martin,[88] Portalié,[89] Mausbach,[90] Montgomery,[91] Hatzfeld,[92] and Bret [93] have written to defend the *Confessions* and the traditional view. The book, however, which is hailed [94] as most authoritative on this side of the question is that of Boyer: *Christianisme et Néo-Platonisme dans la formation de saint Augustin* (Paris 1920). This book has been criticised, not unfairly, by one who shared the same opinion as Boyer, but approached the problem from a different angle. To Nörregaard [95] Boyer seems to be too intent on proving the accuracy of the traditional view; not to put the questions involved sharply enough; to be too indecisive; and to have given a presentation of the problem which is at once unsatisfactory in its methodological principles and psychologically incompetent. We can testify for ourselves that Boyer's analysis of the *Contra Academicos*—an analysis in which he places not a little confidence [96]—reduces the distinct Neo-Platonic tone of the prefaces almost to vanishing point, and ignores some of the really difficult and important passages.[97]

We shall make it clear that Augustine's acceptance of Christianity in 386 was sincere, full, and as it is (rhetoric apart) represented in the *Confessions*. In fact, the correspondence between the *Contra Academicos* and the *Confessions* will be seen to be remarkable.[98] It will also be shown that Augustine at this time was deeply impressed by Neo-Platonism, and felt that he could make a synthesis be-

tween it and the Christian teaching.[99] We must not distort
our view by allowing to intrude into the picture either our
own realization of the impossibility of such a synthesis, or
Augustine's own later repudiation of the Neo-Platonists.
To the Church he looked as to an authority which he could
always obey, and he accepted the mysteries of the Incarnation and the Trinity. To Neo-Platonism he looked for
the rational explanation of everything. He wished not
merely to believe, but to understand. He was persuaded—
and this is the nerve of the whole matter—that as God was
the source of both the way of reason and the way of authority, there could be no possible conflict between these
two ways.[100] Authority was definitely represented by the
Catholic Church. Reason seemed to lie with the Neo-Platonists, although he did not subscribe to everything that
they said.[101] From the way of authority he would never
depart.

B. *Plotinus* [102] or *Porphyry?* [103]

The second problem has arisen in an acute form only
recently. While supposing that Plotinus was the main
source of Augustine's Neo-Platonism at this time, scholars
had usually indicated Augustine's indebtedness to other
Neo-Platonists also. There was a tendency to underrate
other than strictly Plotinian influences; this, for instance,
is seen in the case of Alfaric.[104] In 1933 W. Theiler published his *Porphyrios und Augustin,*[105] in which he tried to
justify the conclusion that almost everything philosophical in Augustine is taken from Porphyry.[106] This was certainly going too far. Henry [107] replied, but erred in the
other direction. According to him there is no trace of Porphyry in the Augustine of this period at all.[108]

It will be seen from our observations on the text that both Plotinus [109] and Porphyry [110] are well represented in the *Contra Academicos*. Of the two, Porphyry seems to have played, as far as the evidence of this work goes, the more important, and what seems to have been a decisive, role.

5

THE HISTORICITY OF *THE DIALOGUES OF CASSICIACUM*

The question of the historicity of the *Contra Academicos* and the other dialogues with which it is inextricably bound up should be discussed at this point. It is of peculiar interest in this case because, as we have seen, many scholars maintain that these dialogues are more trustworthy, are more "historical" than the *Confessions*. Augustine himself claims in the course of the dialogues that they are absolutely faithful in their recorded report of what happened.[111] It is to be noted that this precise claim is made only *in* the dialogues, and that this procedure, as an attempt to achieve verisimilitude, is quite usual even in dialogues that are entirely fictional. Moreover, a close analysis of the dialogues in question will convince the student that they are certainly not entirely historical, however much they may seem to be. It will be necessary to review some of the evidence for and against the historicity of the dialogues before we shall be in a position to draw the conclusion warranted by the facts. Ohlmann,[112] Van Haeringen,[113] Hirzel,[114] among others,[115] have examined this question.

A. *The Evidence in Favour of Historicity*

The great champions of the historicity of the dialogues
are Ohlmann and Van Haeringen. Indeed the scholars
who attack the *Confessions* depend largely upon their
work.[116] Hence it is desirable to discuss their views. Their
position is in no sense subtle. They maintain that these
dialogues are quite new in their *genre:* the conversations
did take place; they were duly recorded by secretaries
present at the debates; we are presented with faithful—
apart from stylistic modifications and omissions—reports
of disputations actually held. In short, what we read was
in each case actually said by the person to whom it is
attributed, although not perhaps in the same form of
words, or in such a summary manner. There was no fiction
employed, or practically none.[117]

Ohlmann brings forward the strongest piece of evidence
in favour of this view. It is the testimony from the *Retractations*,[118] a work written at the very end of his life by
Augustine and specifically intended to correct any misleading impressions or statements given in his other works.
Augustine there pronounces that the *De beata vita,* one
of the *Dialogues of Cassiciacum,* gives a sufficiently reliable picture of what happened in a particular instance:
*librum De beata vita non post libros De Academicis, sed
inter illos ut scriberem contigit. Ex occasione quippe ortus
est diei natalis mei tridui disputatione conpletus, sicut
satis ipse indicat. In quo libro constitit inter nos, qui simul
quaerebamus, non esse beatam vitam nisi perfectam cog-
nitionem dei.* The operative phrase is *sicut satis ipse
indicat.* The dialogue in question is sufficiently reliable.

From this it follows that the others, too, including the *Contra Academicos,* are equally reliable.[119]

Bindemann [120] had already used another argument put forward by Ohlmann. If the dialogues are not what they profess to be, that is, touched-up records of actual conversations, then we must conclude that Augustine's first attempts in the dialogue form were not successful.[121] Ohlmann analyses the argument of the *De ordine,* and demonstrates that the dialogue is from an artistic point of view a failure. Augustine could not have invented it. It must have happened so! It is a new kind of dialogue— a "real" one! [122]

Ohlmann urges, too, that the contrast between the *Contra Academicos, De beata vita,* and *De ordine* on the one hand, and the *Soliloquia* and other dialogues of this period on the other, while it makes the fictional character of the latter appear very clearly, makes the historical character of the former obvious.[123]

Finally, both Ohlmann and Van Haeringen can point to the actual days on which the various discussions in the dialogues took place—a strong testimony to their historicity. It is difficult for a third person to present this argument, for the simple reason that Ohlmann and Van Haeringen give differing accounts of the order of occurrence of the discussions. Either the indications within the dialogues are not consistent, or are difficult to interpret, or one of the scholars has erred. Another possible explanation—that the indications, being fictional, are worthless— will be urged shortly. In the meantime it will be useful to give the two orders of occurrence of the same events as suggested by Ohlmann and Van Haeringen:

Ohlmann [124]	
Date (A.D. 386)	Dialogue
November 10	*Contra Academicos* 1. 5-11
" 11	" " 1.11-16
" 12	" " 1.16-25
" 13	*De beata vita* 7-17
" 14	" " " 17-23
" 15	" " " 23-36
" 16	*De ordine* 1. 6-27
" 17	" " 1.27-33
" 18, 19	....
" 20	*Contra Academicos* 2.10-14; 14-24
" 21	" " 2.25-30
" 22	" " 3. 1-7; 7-45
" 23 (or so)	*De ordine* 2. 1-19; 19-54

Tillemont [125] had suggested this order, but according to him the discussions started on November the 9th. Knöll [126] follows Ohlmann.

Van Haeringen [127]

Van Haeringen's scheme is an attempt to overcome the difficulties besetting Ohlmann's suggested order. He distinguishes between the order of occurrence of the disputations, and the order of composition of the published works. He does not assign dates. His solution had already been rejected by Tillemont.[128]

Order of Occurrence	Order of Composition
Contra Academicos 1	*Contra Academicos* 1
" " 2, 3	*De beata vita*
De ordine 1	*De ordine* 1, 2
De beata vita	*Contra Academicos* 2, 3
De ordine 2	

Van Haeringen's only other serious contribution is his emphasis upon the internal claims of the dialogues on the point that a secretary, *notarius,* was present at the disputations taking down a faithful report.[129] He admits—indeed supposes—that Augustine made some alterations in the style of the record.[130] But the historicity is guaranteed.

B. *The Evidence Against Historicity*

Before passing on to the evidence, it is as well to state that those who argue against the historicity of the dialogues do not deny that some or many of the events described did take place. What they do deny is that every detail is historical and that the dialogues are entirely trustworthy. What is said may be true, but you cannot be sure of it. Hirzel's attitude is precisely this.[131]

It is comparatively easy to dispose of the arguments of Ohlmann, Van Haeringen, and those that follow them.

To admit, as Ohlmann does,[132] that Augustine omitted, changed, or contracted anything in the alleged records of the debates, even though the matter be very slight, does away with the absolute historicity of the dialogues.[133] If Augustine allowed himself one change, he very likely allowed himself many.[134] One has no longer any control over the historicity.

The text from the *Retractations* [135] is of little use on the question as a whole. It is to be noted that Augustine says there that he wrote *(scriberem)* the book; that the *book* was begun on his birthday and was finished in a three-day disputation *(disputatio,* a term which may refer to an actual debate or equally well to a literary form; [136] the same remark is valid for the term *quaerebamus* [137]);

and that the book itself indicates *these* (*sicut*) circumstances—but not necessarily any others—reasonably well
(*satis*). It must be emphasized that in the very word
(*satis*) that guarantees the historicity of two particular
points, there is a warning that the other details recounted
in the book may *not* be historical. Augustine clearly implies that one cannot take everything as stated. The argument based on the assumption that Augustine could not
write a poor dialogue [138] is, of course, quite useless. Why
could not Augustine fail? There is every indication that
he was dissatisfied with his efforts. In the *Contra Academicos* he changes over from question and answer to a
set speech.[139] The dialogues composed by him shortly afterwards dispense with all verisimilitude, and in the *Retractations* [140] he notes that he improved in the technique of
writing through the process of writing. Augustine admits
that he learnt from his mistakes. Why should we deny
that he made any? Again, to assert that the later dialogues
of Augustine are fictional—as they certainly are—does not
prove that the earlier ones are not fictional. And the whole
force—if there is any—of the argument from the possibility of assigning dates and order of occurrence of the
dialogues is obviously vitiated by the contradictions of the
accounts. There are many serious difficulties against the
reconstructions of both Ohlmann [141] and Van Haeringen.[142] In any case a fictional dialogué could—and
usually attempts to—be consistent in details such as dates.

But, apart from the inadequacy of what has been urged
in its favour, there are weighty reasons for arguing against
the absolute historicity of the dialogues.

The first objection arises naturally from the form in
which the works are written—the dialogue form.[143] In

composing [144] and publishing [145] these works Augustine
deliberately chose [146] a particular literary *genre* and did
not fail to employ all the devices to be found in the many
models that were available. We can trace how closely his
dialogues approach to these models, and the measure of
their approximation is, to some extent, a measure of their
untrustworthiness as guaranteeing facts.[147] There is, then:
(1) The division of the works into *books*.[148] (2) A *preface*
to some of these books, and in the case of *Contra Academicos 1* a preface taking the form of an introductory letter
addressed to the person to whom the work is dedicated: [149]
it is lengthy, and partly autobiographical, and also ex-
horts, as is the way in such protreptics,[150] the addressee to
the study of philosophy, and the adoption of a "way of
life." (3) A *mis-en-scène* which accords exactly with all
the usual requirements of a "school-room" dialogue: [151]
the reference to a preceding discussion,[152] the determining
of what is to be discussed at the next session,[153] the summary of what has been said in the absence of one of the
interlocutors,[154] the presence of a master and disciples,[155]
the appointment of an arbiter,[156] and the expression of
astonishment when one of the disciples gives a view which
would seem to be far beyond his powers.[157] (4) The usual
guarantee in such dialogues that the discussions did take
place, and that the report presented is faithful even to the
extent of noting when an interlocutor departed or returned, and of quoting exact words—such accuracy being
said to be founded on the taking of notes during the discussions.[158] (5) The traditional range of *topics* discussed in
such dialogues, not only with regard to such questions as
knowledge, happiness, and the order of the universe, but
also such details as are common in the spiritual-guide-and-

disciple type of dialogue: the soul's return to God, the necessity to know oneself and God, the importance of revelation, the motifs of philosophy as a harbour, of corporal life as life in a prison, of the activity of demon-spirits of the air, of the masses who are sunk in ignorance and the few that are wise, and so on. (6) Finally, some lesser details which are commonly found in dialogues: the occasion of the dialogue being a birthday or some feast,[159] the attribution of inspiration and "possession" to one of the interlocutors,[160] the recognition that one's argument will be refuted at some other time by some person wiser than oneself,[161] and a concluding prayer to a deity.[162]

A second argument against the absolute historicity of the dialogues is suggested by the change from the dialectical method of enquiry to what amounts almost to a formal lecture—a change which takes place both in the *Contra Academicos* and the *De ordine*.[163] Augustine was not the only one to find it difficult to sustain the dramatic interest that we find in Plato's dialogues,[164] and it was only natural that the "Aristotelian" dialogue of set speeches became the usual type. These are to be seen, for example, in the works of Cicero. Augustine may have tried to imitate Plato, and found that he could not do it. The first book of the *Contra Academicos*, for instance, makes an honest attempt at being dialectical, of proceeding by question and answer, but it fails notably to stir one's interest or advance the argument. It is only in the third book when set speeches are introduced that something is achieved. In the *Contra Academicos* one such speech extends to one third of the length of the whole work. The introduction of a speech running to some six thousand words without interruption cannot but shake our confidence in the historicity claimed for it. In this matter we cannot ignore the fact that, having completed the *Dialogues of Cassiciacum,* Augustine never again attempted dialogues either in the Platonic or Aristotelian manner; his other dialogues are in the form of a catechism, and make no claim to historicity. It may have been that the effort to convey "actuality" was profitless and troublesome.[165]

A third difficulty is concerned with the complete improbability of certain episodes alleged to have taken place. Even the exponents of the view that the dialogues are historical allow that one or two things may have been invented. Ohlmann, following Kaibel, is prepared to admit that the activities of the mouse in *De ordine* 1. 6, 9 may have been invented.[166] Van Haeringen, following Thimme, admits that some of the views attributed to Trygetius could scarcely have been his very own.[167] This whole section of the *De ordine* (1. 5-22) seems to the present writer to strain credulity far beyond the breaking point. No analysis can succeed in conveying the impression of unreality the reading of this particular text itself imparts. It is certainly invented. And if this is invented, what confidence can we have in the historicity of the *Dialogues of Cassiciacum?* [168]

C. *Conclusion on the Question of Historicity*

It is admitted by all that the *Dialogues of Cassiciacum* are not entirely fictional; they are to some extent, at any rate, related to facts. The interlocutors were such as they are represented as being, and at the time in question were actually in Cassiciacum, and were engaged in such exercises as are described in the *Dialogues.* This much can be accepted on the testimony of the *Letters* and *Confessions*. The *Retractations*, moreover, almost certainly guarantee the historicity of two details from the *De beata vita*. From this we may suppose that other details may be historical, especially details found in the introductions to the books [169]—unless we find conflicting evidence elsewhere.

But the *Dialogues of Cassiciacum* are emphatically not to receive our trust, and their evidence is not to be preferred to that of the *Confessions*,[170] for instance, if there is a conflict (but there is not [171]), merely because they *claim* to be historical. They are the written compositions of Augustine, and consciously and closely follow both as to form and matter previous models. The internal assurances as to their historicity are worthless.

It is impossible to assess the extent to which fiction may have been employed. Very much may have been invented. It is evident that the element of fiction is far from being negligible.

*   *   *

The text of the *Contra Academicos* used for the present translation is that of Pius Knöll in the *Corpus scriptorum ecclesiasticorum latinorum*, vol. 63 (Vienna-Leipzig 1922). Knöll's work has been criticised by de Labriolle, Jolivet, and Henry among others.[172] Nevertheless, his text is sufficiently superior to that of the Benedictines (Migne, *Patrologia latina* 32.905-958) to be preferred to it.

I list three recent translations, the last two of which I have seen:

Garvey, M. P., *Saint Augustine, Against the Academicians* (Milwaukee 1942).

Jolivet, R., *Contre les Académiciens,* in *Oeuvres de saint Augustin, 1*ʳᵉ *série: Opuscules 4, Dialogues philosophiques 1: Problèmes fondamentaux* (Paris 1939).

Kavanagh, D. J., *Answer to Skeptics. A Translation of St. Augustine's Contra Academicos* (New York 1943).

BOOK ONE

Truth and Happiness

CHAPTER 1

Preface

I wish,[1] Romanianus,[2] that Virtue, who never allows fortune[3] to take anyone away from her, could, for her part, snatch[4] from fortune, resist as she might, the man that is suited to her purpose. If that could be, she certainly would already have placed her hands upon you. She would have proclaimed you her own by right; and putting you in possession of wealth that is truly secure, she would not suffer you to depend on chance, even if it favoured you. But the fact is that, whether because we have deserved it, or because this is necessary by nature,[5] the divine[6] spirit[7] that is united to our mortal bodies can never reach the harbour[8] of wisdom, where the wind of fortune, favourable or unfavourable, cannot reach it, unless fortune herself, good or bad—but only seeming so—bring it thither. Accordingly, we can do nothing for you but pray, so that by our prayers we may win, if we can, the favour from that God who has a care of these things that He bring you back to your true self[9]—and in doing so He will likewise bring you back to us—and allow your mind, which for so long has yearned for respite, to emerge at length into the fresh air of true freedom.

35

Indeed, it may be that what is commonly called "fortune" is governed by a secret ordinance; and we call "chance" that element in things for which we can offer no cause or reason; [10] and nothing is either helpful or harmful to the part which does not turn out to be helpful to, and fit in with, the whole. [11] It is this thought, proposed in declarations of doctrines most fruitful and far removed from the understanding of the uninitiated, [12] which that philosophy [13] to which I call you promises to make clear to her true devotees. Do not, therefore, think too little of yourself, merely because it is your lot to have to put up with many things unworthy of your spirit. For if divine providence [14] has a care for us—which we have no reason to doubt—then, believe me, you are treated as it is right that you should be treated. You were born, for instance, into this earthly life, abounding as it does in all error, with such talent—obvious even from your earliest youth when reason's progress is but weak and faltering—as always makes me marvel. Riches were showered upon you from every side, and these riches had already begun to overwhelm in the tides of pleasure your spirit and your youth which eagerly sought whatever seemed beautiful and good. It was then, just when you were on the point of sinking, that those winds of fortune which are commonly regarded as being adverse, snatched you away.

2. Certainly, if in giving to our citizens bear fights and spectacles such as were never seen by them before, you were always received with the most enthusiastic applause of the whole gathering; if you were praised to the skies by the unanimous and united cries of foolish men, of which the number is very great; if no one ever dared to risk your

displeasure; if municipal records were to signalize in bronze that you are a patron not only of the citizens but also of the neighbouring peoples; if they erected statues of you, heaped honours upon you, and even invested you with powers greater than is customary in municipal appointments; if your table were sumptuously laden for banquests every day; if any man might confidently ask of you and be assured of receiving whatever he needed or his fastidiousness desired, and if many benefits were lavished even upon such as did not ask for them; if your estate itself, carefully and faithfully administered by your own people, were sufficiently large and organized to meet such great expenses; and if, meanwhile, you yourself were to pass your time in exquisite mansions, in splendid baths, occupying yourself with games of dice such as honour does not forbid, with hunting, and with feasting; if your clients, your fellow citizens, if, in fine, throngs of people kept on pronouncing you as a most kind person, most generous, most elegant, and most fortunate: would anyone, Romanianus, I ask you, would any one dare to mention to you another happiness—happiness which alone is happiness? Who could then persuade you that not only were you not happy, but that you were especially unhappy in not having the faintest realization that you were unhappy? [15] But now, how quickly you have been made to realize this by the many great reverses that you have endured! Obviously, there is now no need to instance the experiences of others in order to convince you how fleeting, unreliable, and full of misery is all that which mortals think to be good. Indeed, your own experience has been such as we can use in order to convince others.

3. That part [16] of you, then, because of which you have ever sought after what was honourable and good; because of which you have preferred to be generous rather than wealthy; because of which you have never desired power at the expense of justice; because of which you have never yielded to adversity or dishonesty; that divine element, I say, which has somehow been lulled to sleep in you by the drowsy lethargy of this life, providence, working in secret, has decided to rouse by means of the several harsh buffetings which you have suffered.

Wake up! [17] wake up! I beg you. Believe me, you will be heartily glad that this world has scarcely flattered you at all with its gifts and successes by which the unwary are ensnared. I myself had almost been trapped by these things, preaching them to others, as I did, had not some chest trouble compelled me to give up my profession of windy rhetoric and take refuge in the lap of philosophy. She now nourishes and cherishes me in that leisure which we have so much desired. She has freed me entirely from that heresy [18] into which I had precipitated you with myself. For she teaches, and teaches truly, that nothing whatever that is discerned by mortal eyes, or is the object of any perception, should be worshipped, but that everything such should be contemned.[19] She promises to make known clearly the true and hidden God and is on the very point of deigning to present Him to our view—as it were, through shining clouds.

4. Our Licentius shares with great enthusiasm this way of life with me. He has been so entirely converted to it from the seductions and pleasures dear to youth that I feel confident in daring to propose him for his father's

imitation. I speak of philosophy from whose breasts no age can complain that it is excluded. And so that I may incite you all the more eagerly to cling to her and drink of her—although I have long been aware of your great thirst for her—I have decided to send you a foretaste. It will, I hope—and I beg that my hope be not in vain—be sweet, and, as it were, an enticement to you.

Here, then, I have enclosed a written version of a discussion between Trygetius and Licentius. For the young man first mentioned, as a result of his short experience of military life undertaken with a view to overcoming his distaste for study, is now with us again and is most eager and greedy for profound and serious enquiry. A very few days, therefore, after we had come to live in the country, when I was exhorting and encouraging them to the pursuit of study and noticed that they were more prepared than I had expected and full of enthusiasm, I decided to find out what ability they had for their age, especially since the *Hortensius*,[20] a book of Cicero's, seemed already for the most part to have won them over to philosophy. Accordingly, I engaged a stenographer,[21] so that:

> . . . the winds might not scatter our labour,[22]

and I allowed nothing to be lost. In this book, then, you will read the points and opinions put forward by them and also the things said by Alypius and myself.

CHAPTER 2

The Problem

5. When, therefore, at my invitation and at a time which seemed suitable, we had all come together in one place for this purpose, I said: "Do you doubt at all that we ought to know truth?"

"Certainly not," said Trygetius, and the others indicated by their expression that they agreed.

"And if," said I, "we can be happy without knowing truth, would you still think that the knowledge of truth is necessary?"

At this point Alypius intervened: "I think it better," he said, "that I act as arbiter in this question. For since I have decided to go to the city, it is better that I be not asked to defend a side; and, moreover, I can more easily delegate to another the role of arbiter than that of defender in the discussion. Wherefore, from now on do not expect from me any contribution to either side."

When all had acceded to his request, and I had repeated my question, Trygetius said: "We wish to be happy,[23] that is certain; and if this is something we can arrive at without truth, we need not seek truth."

"What is that?" I said. "Is it your opinion that we can be happy even though we have not found truth?"

Here Licentius interposed: "Yes, if we seek truth."

When I indicated to the others that I wished to know what they thought, Navigius said: "What Licentius has

said makes me think.   Perhaps indeed that very thing, to
live in the search for truth, could be happiness."

"Well, then," said Trygetius, "define happiness, so that
I may gather from your definition what I ought to reply."

"What else do you think happiness is," said I, "but to
live in conformity with that which is best in man?" [24]

"Let me not use words loosely," Trygetius said; "I think
you should define for me what that term 'best' means."

"Who," said I, "would think that anything else is best
in man but that part of his spirit whose commands whatever else there is in man must obey? And this part, lest
you ask for another definition, can be termed 'mind' or
'reason.' But if this does not appear acceptable to you, ask
yourself how you would define either happiness or that
which is best in man."

"I am in agreement," he replied.

6. "Now, then," said I, "to return to the proposition:
do you think that one can be happy without finding truth,
provided only one seek for it?"

He replied: "I repeat my opinion already given.[25] I do
not think it possible at all."

"And you others," I said, "what is your opinion?"

"I think it quite possible," Licentius said. "Our fore-
bears, for instance, whom we know to have been wise and
happy, were happy and good for the sole reason that they
were seeking truth." [26]

"I am grateful," said I, "that you made me judge [27]
along with Alypius, whom, I must confess, I had already
begun to envy. Since, therefore, one of you holds that
happiness is possible in the mere seeking for truth, and the
other, that it is possible only in the finding of it, and Navi-

gius a moment ago indicated that he wishes to take his stand on your side, Licentius, I am quite eager to see how you will be able to defend your opinions. The question is an important one and deserves serious discussion."

"If it is a matter of importance," said Licentius, "it calls for discussion by men of importance."

"Do not look," I replied, "especially here in this villa, for what is difficult to find anywhere in the world. But tell us rather why you have given what, I think, is not an ill-considered opinion, and how you understand it. Surely, too, experience shows that when men of little moment apply themselves to great matters, these matters lend greatness to them."

CHAPTER 3

Is the Mere Search for Truth Sufficient for Happiness?

7. "I perceive," said Licentius, "that you are doing your best to make us argue the question with one another, and, I am sure, you do so with some good purpose in mind. Let me ask, then, why cannot a man be happy who seeks for truth, even though he never find it?"

"Because," replied Trygetius, "a happy man as we conceive him must be a wise man,[28] perfect in all things. But one who is still seeking, is not perfect. I cannot, then, for the life of me see how you can assert that such a man is happy."

To which the other replied: "Does the authority of the ancients mean anything to you?"

"Not of all of them," said Trygetius.

"Whose authority, then?"

"The authority, of course, of those who were wise."

"Carneades—" asked Licentius, "would you not think him wise?"

"I am not a Greek," answered the other. "I do not know who this Carneades was." [29]

"Well, then," said Licentius, "what about our own renowned Cicero? What do you think of him?"

After a prolonged silence, the other replied: "He was a wise man."

"In that case," said Licentius, "his opinion on the point at issue has some weight with you, has it not?"

"It has," was the reply.

"Listen to it, then, for I think that you have forgotten it. It was Cicero's opinion that a man is happy if he seeks for truth, even though he should never be able to find it." [30]

"Where," asked Trygetius, "has Cicero said this?"

"Who does not know," Licentius rejoined, "that he affirmed most strongly that man could perceive nothing, and that nothing is left to the wise man to do but to seek diligently for truth, because, if he were to give assent to uncertainties, even though perhaps they were in fact true, he would have no guarantee against error. And to be in error is the greatest fault in one who is wise.[31] Accordingly, if we must believe that the wise man is necessarily happy, and that wisdom has its perfection in the mere seeking for truth, why do we hesitate to believe that happiness itself can be achieved in the mere search for truth?"

8. The other in his turn asked: "Well, now, may I return to something which I conceded without giving it sufficient thought?"

Here I intervened: "People who enter into a discussion in order to give a childish exhibition of their intelligence, and not through any desire of finding truth, do not usually allow such a request. But I not only allow the request—and that all the more as you are still in need of formation and instruction—but it is my wish that you make it a rule that you ought to return to the discussion of such points as you have granted on too little reflection."

Licentius, too, remarked: "I think we have real progress in philosophy when a disputant thinks little of victory as compared with the discovery of what is just and true. Accordingly, I am glad to defer to your rules and advice, and allow—for this matter is for me to decide—Trygetius to go back to what he thinks he conceded too lightly."

Then Alypius said: "You yourselves agree with me that the time has not yet come for me to exercise the powers of the office entrusted to me. But since the journey which I have planned for some time compels me to break away, my associate judge will not refuse to take my place and exercise a double power until my return. Indeed, I can see that this discussion between you is going to last for a good while."

When he had left, Licentius asked: "What was it that you conceded too lightly? Tell us."

He replied: "I too lightly conceded that Cicero was wise."

"So, Cicero was not a wise man, Cicero who not only was the first to treat of philosophy in the Latin tongue, but brought that process to perfection?"

"Even though I should grant him to be wise," said he, "that does not mean that I approve of everything he said."

"Well, now, you will have to disprove many other propositions of his if you are to escape seeming impertinent in attacking the proposition in question!"

"What if I am prepared to assert that this was the only point on which he was not right? So far as I can see, what concerns you is the weight of the reasons which I bring forward to clinch my argument—and that only."

"Go on," said the other, "what can I do to oppose him who proclaims that he opposes Cicero?"

9. Whereupon Trygetius said: "I wish that you who act as judge would consider how you defined happiness earlier on: you said that he is happy who lives in conformity with that part of his spirit which, as is right, should govern the other parts. As for you, Licentius, I wish you would concede to me—for I have through that freedom which especially philosophy promises to win for us, thrown off the yoke of authority—that the man who still seeks truth is not perfect."

After a long silence, the other replied: "No, I do not make that concession."

"Why?" asked Trygetius. "Explain yourself. I am all ears and am dying to hear how it is possible that a man can be perfect while still seeking truth."

"I agree," said he, "that one who has not arrived at his goal is not perfect. But it is my opinion that only God, or perhaps the soul of man once it has abandoned this body, this dark prison house,[32] can know the truth of which we speak. Man's end, however, is perfectly to seek the truth. Our ideal indeed is perfection—a perfection, however, which is proper to man."

"In that case," said Trygetius, "man cannot be happy. How could he be, if he cannot achieve that which he earnestly desires? But the fact is that man's life can be happy, since he can live in conformity with that part of his spirit, which, it is right, should govern in man. Therefore, he can find truth. Otherwise, his only course is to get a grip on himself and refuse to desire truth so that, since he cannot possess it, he may thus avoid being of necessity unhappy."

"But this precisely is happiness for man," said the other, "perfectly to seek truth; for this is to reach the end beyond which one cannot go. That man, therefore, who is less persistent in the search for truth than he ought to be, does not arrive at the end of man. Whereas he who devotes himself as much as a man can, and ought, to the finding of truth, even if he does not find it, is happy. He accomplishes all that he was born to accomplish. If he fail to find truth, the failure is because nature has refused the favour. Finally, since man must of necessity be either happy or unhappy, is it not sheer madness to say that that man is unhappy who, as far as he can, is active by day and by night in the search for truth? He must, therefore, be happy. So, it seems to me that our definition of happiness is more in favour of my view. For if that man is happy, as indeed he is, who lives in conformity with that part of his spirit which rightly governs the other parts, and that part is called 'reason,' then let me ask if a man who perfectly seeks truth does not live according to 'reason'? Since it is ridiculous to hesitate, why do we not say that man is happy in the mere search for truth?"

CHAPTER 4

What is Error?

10. "For my part," said Trygetius, "the man who is in error seems to me neither to live in conformity with reason nor to be in any way happy. And everyone who ever seeks and never finds, is in error. Hence, you must prove either of two things: that a man who is in error can be happy; or that he who never finds what he seeks, is not in error."

"One who is happy cannot be in error," Licentius replied. When he had remained silent for a long time, he said: "One who seeks is not in error, because he is seeking precisely that he may not err."

Then Trygetius said: "True it is, he is seeking so that he may not err; but he is in error when he does not find what he seeks. You counted his unwillingness to err as an argument in your favour—as though no one were ever in error against his will, or as if there were anyone at all who errs without doing so against his will!"

When Licentius was at a loss for a long time what he should say in reply, I intervened: "You must define what error is. Obviously, now that you have penetrated deeply into it, you can see its distinguishing marks more readily."

"I," said Licentius, "cannot define anything, even though it be easier to define error than to confine it."

"I," said the other, "shall define it without any trouble at all—not by reason of any mental acumen, but because of the strength of my case. For, assuredly, to be in error is *ever to seek and never to find.*"

"If I," said Licentius, "could with any ease refute even that definition, I should have ceased long ago to fail in support of my case. But either the matter is in itself difficult, or it appears so to me; wherefore, I beg of you to adjourn the discussion until tomorrow morning. As you see, though I have thought the matter over carefully, I cannot think of anything to reply today."

I decided that his request should be granted, and the others agreed. We got up and walked about, talking of a great variety of things, while he remained absorbed in thought. When he saw how vain his efforts were, he decided to give his mind a rest and join in our conversation. Later on when evening came, they wanted to return to the old battle, but I calmed them down and persuaded them to agree to adjourn the discussion to some other day. Then we went to the baths.

11. On the following day when we had sat down together, I said: "Take up what you began yesterday."

Licentius replied: "If I am not mistaken, the discussion was adjourned at my request, because the definition of error proved too difficult for me."

"In that," said I, "it is clear that you are not in error and I would heartily wish that this might be a good omen [33] for you of what is to come."

"Listen, then," he said, "I would have given this definition yesterday also, if you had not intervened. Error, in my opinion, is *the approbation as true of what is not true;* and a man who thinks that truth is always to be sought for, can in no way fall into this: he who approves of nothing, cannot approve of what is not true. Therefore, he cannot be in error. But it is very easy for him to be happy.

I shall not have to go far to show you how. If we ourselves could pass every day as we passed yesterday, I can
see no reason why we should hesitate to call ourselves
happy. For we passed the time in great peace of mind,
keeping our spirit free from every defilement of the body,[34]
and far removed from the burning flames of all desires.
We cultivated 'reason' to the best of human capability,
that is, we lived in conformity with that divine part of
the spirit; and this we agreed in our definition of yesterday is happiness.

And yet, so far as I know, we found nothing. We only
sought for truth. Man can, then, be happy in the mere
search for truth, even though he can never find it. And
as for your definition, note how easily it is proved wrong
by a simple consideration. You said that to be in error was
ever to seek and never to find. Suppose that a man is not
seeking anything and is asked, for example, if it is now
daytime, and without due reflection at once conjectures
that it is nighttime and replies to that effect, do you not
think that that man is in error? Your definition, then, has
not embraced even this monstrous kind of error. And if,
in addition, it has embraced those who are not in error,
could any definition be worse? If a man, for instance, were
going to Alexandria and were going by the direct road,
you could not, I take it, say that he was one who was in
error. But if, meeting with various obstacles, he should
spend a long time upon the way and should be overtaken,
while still on the journey, by death, has that man not
always sought and never found and still was not in error?"

"He did not always seek," said Trygetius.

12.   "You are right," said Licentius, "and your remark

is to the point, for now your definition is shown to be absolutely irrelevant. Certainly, it was not I who said that he was happy who always sought for truth. That a man should always seek for truth is not possible: first, because a man does not exist always; secondly, because when he does begin to be a man, he cannot then proceed to seek for truth. He is prevented by his age. Or, if you understand by 'always' that he allows no time to be lost in which he can in fact perform the act of seeking, you must then go back again to the road to Alexandria! Suppose that a man from the time when he is not prevented either by age or commitments from undertaking the journey, sets out upon that way and, as I said above, although he at no point leaves the straight road,[35] nevertheless dies before he can reach his destination: you will certainly be greatly in error, if you think that he was in error, although during all the time he could, he never ceased to seek and yet never found the end of his journey. Consequently, if my account is true; and if in accordance with it that man is not in error who, even though he does not find truth, seeks for it to the end, and is happy because he lives in conformity with 'reason'; and if your definition is refuted and should not, even if it were not refuted, engage my attention any further, if only because by my own definition my case has been upheld: why, I ask you, have we not already ceased from this discussion?"

CHAPTER 5

What is wisdom?

13.   Trygetius resumed: "Do you concede that wisdom is *the right way of life?*"

"Yes, I do not doubt that," replied Licentius; "but all the same, I would like you to define wisdom for me, so that I may know whether your notion of it is the same as mine."

The other asked: "Is it not sufficiently defined for you in the terms of my question? You have already conceded what I wanted. For unless I am mistaken, it is correct to call wisdom *the right way of life.*" [36]

"Nothing," said Licentius, "seems more ridiculous to me than that definition."

"That may be," replied Trygetius, "but go easy, please. Think before you laugh. Nothing is more contemptible than a laugh which rightly deserves to be laughed at."

"But do you not agree," said Licentius, "that death is the contrary of life?"

"I do," said the other.

"In that case," said Licentius, "it seems to me that nothing better deserves to be called *the way of life* than that way by which one takes steps to avoid death."

Trygetius agreed.

"Therefore, if a traveller in order to avoid a side road which, he has heard, is infested with brigands, continues straight along the highroad and thus avoids death, has he not followed *the way of life,* and that, too, *the right way of life?* And nobody calls that 'wisdom.' How, then, can wisdom be every *right way of life?* I conceded only that wisdom was *a* right way of life though not the *only* one. Your definition should not embrace anything irrelevant. Therefore, if you please, try again. What in your opinion is wisdom?"

14. Trygetius was silent for a long time. Then he said: "Well, if you have made up your mind never to put an end to this question, I give you this other definition. Wisdom is *the right way of life that leads to truth.*"

"It is the same story over again," replied the other. "This definition also refutes itself. To illustrate: when according to Virgil, Aeneas had been told by his mother:

'Proceed and direct your footsteps where the way leads you,' [37]

following this way he arrived where he had been told, that is, at truth. Maintain, if you care to, that where he as he walked, put his foot, can be called wisdom. But I am very foolish, indeed, in trying to refute your description of wisdom, since no other is more favourable to my cause. For you said, not that wisdom is truth itself, but that it is *the way that leads to truth.* Whoever, therefore, uses this way, by that very fact uses wisdom; and he who uses wisdom, is necessarily wise. Hence, he will be wise who perfectly seeks truth, even though he has not arrived at it. In fact, as I see it, *the way that leads to truth* is best understood to be the diligent search for truth. Using this way alone, then, he will already be wise, and no wise man is unhappy. Every man, however, must be either happy or unhappy. Wherefore, not only the finding of truth, but also the search itself, and by itself, for truth, will make him happy."

15. Trygetius smiled and resumed: "I deserve that this should happen to me, since I have imprudently agreed with my adversary on a side issue. As if I were expert in defining! Or as if there were anything, in my opinion, more futile in discussion! Would there ever be an end if I were again to ask you for a definition [38] of something, and then, pretending that I did not follow anything you said, if I were to demand a definition of the words of that definition, and so on of every single word that would be employed as a consequence? If it is right to demand from me a definition of wisdom, then will it not be right for me to demand a definition even of what is most obvious? Is there any word of which nature has imprinted in our spirit a clearer notion than that word 'wisdom'? I do admit, however, that once the notion itself leaves as it were the harbour of our mind and spreads the sails of words, immediately it is menaced a thousand times with the shipwreck of misrepresentation. Accordingly, let there be no definition of wisdom demanded, or let our judge be good enough to step down and come to her defence."

At that point, seeing that it was getting too dark to write down the record, and that they were embarking as if anew on a very big subject of discussion, I adjourned the debate until the following day. The sun had already begun to set when we had started the discussion, and we had spent almost the whole day in attending to matters on the farm and in going over the first book of Virgil.

CHAPTER 6

New Definition of Wisdom

16. When it was daylight—for so we had arranged it the day before, in order that we might have plenty of time—immediately we set about the problem which we had put before ourselves. I said: "Yesterday, Trygetius, you asked me to give up being judge and to protect the interests of wisdom—as if wisdom in your discussion actually had any enemy to fear, or, no matter who was defending her, should be in such straits as to be forced to ask for greater assistance.[39] As a matter of fact, the only question which has arisen between you is: 'What is wisdom?' And here neither of you opposes her, for each of you wants her. And if you, Trygetius, think that you have failed in defining wisdom, you should not on that account abandon the remaining defence of your position. And so, I shall give you a definition of wisdom, a definition, however, which is neither mine nor new, but the one given by the men of old;—and I am surprised that you did not remember it. This is not the first time that you have heard that 'wisdom is *the knowledge of things human and divine.*' "[40]

17. Here Licentius, whom I had begun to think would after that definition be at a loss for something to say, immediately added: "Why, then, I ask you, do we not call wise that depraved fellow, who to our own certain knowledge indulges himself in countless debaucheries? I mean the notorious Albicerius, who for many years at Carthage gave some extraordinary and true answers to those who

consulted him. I could give you innumerable instances; but I am talking to people who know all about it for themselves, and a few cases are enough for my purpose." Turning to me, he said: "When a spoon could not be found anywhere in the house, did he not, when I consulted him at your request, not only tell me promptly and accurately what was missing, but also named its owner and where it was hidden? Again, when a slave, as we were going along to consult him, had stolen a certain number of the coins which he was carrying, Albicerius ordered him to count out the full sum, and before our very eyes made the slave return those he had stolen, before he himself had seen the coins or had found out from us how much had been brought for him. I omit the fact that his answer to what we consulted him about was perfectly correct.

18. "And what of the case about which you yourself told us, and which used to cause Flaccianus,[41] a man of distinction and learning, to wonder? He had entered into negotiations about buying a farm, and interviewed our 'prophet' to see if he would be able to tell him what he had been doing. Albicerius immediately told him not only the nature of his business, but also—and this caused Flaccianus to utter loud cries of astonishment—gave even the name of the farm, a name so peculiar that Flaccianus himself could scarcely remember it. And I cannot recall without stupefaction the fact that to a friend of ours, and a disciple of yours who wished to make fun of him in demanding insolently that he should tell him of what he was thinking in his mind, Albicerius replied that he was thinking of a line of Virgil. Amazed, the other could not deny it, but went on to ask what line it was. Albicerius, who

scarcely ever had noticed even in passing the school of a grammarian, gave out the lines glibly without difficulty or hesitation. Does it follow that the things about which he was asked were not things human? Or did he give precise and true answers to those who consulted him without a knowledge of things divine? Either hypothesis is ridiculous. For things human are nothing but the things of men, such as silver, coins, a farm, and, finally, the act of thinking itself. And who would not rightly understand by things divine those things by means of which divination itself comes within man's power? If we agree, then, to the definition of wisdom as *the knowledge of things human and divine,* Albicerius was wise."

CHAPTER 7

19. Trygetius replied: "To begin with, I do not call *that* knowledge in which he who professes it is sometimes deceived. For knowledge is made up of things not only comprehended, but comprehended in such a way that in that knowledge no one should be in error, or should vacillate, no matter what the opposition be. And therefore, some philosophers say with great justice that such knowledge can be found only in the wise man, who should hold that which he defends and admits not only certainly, but also unshakeably.[42] We know, however, that Albicerius whom you mentioned, often said many things that were not true—a fact which I know not only on the information of others, but, being present on one occasion, saw for myself. Shall I, then, say that that man has knowledge,

though he has often said things that were not true, a man whom I would not say had knowledge even if with hesitation he spoke truth? You can take what I say about him as my opinion on haruspices,[48] augurs,[44] all those who consult the stars,[45] and all interpreters of dreams,[46] or you will have to produce, if you can, one of this ilk who upon consultation never was vague in his replies and, as proved by the sequel, never gave an incorrect answer. As for seers,[47] I do not think that I need trouble about them: they speak from the mind of another.

20. "And, though I grant that things human are the things of men, do you think that anything that chance can give or take away from us belongs to us? And when one speaks of the knowledge of human things, does one mean that knowledge through which one knows how many, or what kind of, farms we have, or how much gold, how much silver, or, indeed, what lines of another's poetry we think of in our minds? The real knowledge of human things is that which knows the light of prudence, the beauty of temperance, the strength of fortitude, and the holiness of justice. Verily, these are the things which we can dare to say, without dreading fortune, are truly ours.

"If that fellow Albicerius had learned these, he would never, believe me, have lived in such depravity and debauchery. And the fact that he told his questioner what verse he was thinking of in his mind, even this does not, I think, count among the number of things that are ours. I do not deny that the liberal arts can to a certain extent be possessed by our minds. But even the entirely uneducated has it within his power to recite or declaim a verse belonging to another. It is not strange that such things should come to our minds, considering that they can be perceived also by certain contemptible beings living in the air called 'demons,' [48] who may, I confess, be superior to us in precision and subtlety of the senses, but not, I hold, in reason. This kind of thing comes about in some mysterious way, a way entirely beyond our usual sense perception. If we should wonder at the extraordinary sagacity—in which she is superior to man—with which the tiny bee flies from no matter whence to the place where she has already placed her honey, should we on that account regard her as superior to us, or, at any rate, put her on the same level as ourselves?

21. "And so, I would think more of your Albicerius if, when questioned by one who was eager to learn, he had taught him the art of verse-making itself; or, when invited to do so by one of his clients, had straightway composed verses of his own on a theme proposed to him there and then. This is what Flaccianus himself, as you are accustomed to tell us, often said. He was a man who in his own exalted spirit scorned and derided that kind of divination, and attributed it—so he used to say—to some contemptible sort of being by whose inspiration, as it were, Albicerius was usually filled and prompted so as to be able to give these replies. Man of great learning that he was, he used to ask those who wondered at these replies, if Albicerius could teach grammar or music or geometry. And who that knew the man, could deny that he was entirely ignorant of all such knowledge? Accordingly, Flaccianus most strongly advised those who had acquired this knowledge to elect without any misgiving for the operation of their own spirit over that of such divination, and to do all

they could to prepare and support that mind of theirs with this knowledge. Thus it would be able to rise superior to, and leap beyond, that airy creation of invisible beings.

CHAPTER 8

22. "Now, all agree that things divine are of a much higher order and more sublime than are human things. How, then, could Albicerius have acquired a knowledge of them who knew nothing of his own real nature? He may perhaps have thought that the stars which we see each night, are something great when compared with the true and inscrutable God, who is perhaps—but only rarely—perceived by intelligence, and is never perceived by any sense. The stars, however, are before our very eyes. They are not, therefore, those divine things which wisdom professes that she alone knows. And the other things which are exploited by those so-called diviners, either in order to show off, or to make money, are certainly of less account than the stars. Albicerius, then, had no part in the knowledge of things human and divine, and in vain have you in this way attempted to undermine our definition. Finally, since we should regard whatever does not fall into the categories either of divine or of human things, as most unworthy of our attention, and should altogether contemn it, where, I ask you, is that wise man of yours to seek for truth?"

"In things divine," replied Licentius, "for undoubtedly even in man there is capacity that is divine."

"Does Albicerius, then, already know those things, for

which the wise man of whom you speak will continue always to seek?"

"Yes," said Licentius, "he already knows things divine, but not those which are to be sought for by the wise man. Who could concede to him the power of divination, yet deny to him the possession of things divine, from which *divination* is named, without upsetting all the received conventions of speech? Wherefore, unless I am mistaken, that definition of yours has embraced something other than what pertains to wisdom."

23. Trygetius answered: "He who brought forward that definition will defend it, if he chooses. But now— answer me, so that at long last we may come to the point of the debate."

"I am ready," said Licentius.

"Do you concede," he asked, "that Albicerius knew truth?"

"I do," he said.

"He was better, then, than the wise man you describe."

"Not at all," said the other, "for the kind of truth for which the wise man seeks, is not acquired not only by that raving charlatan, but not even by the wise man as long as he lives in the body. This truth, however, is so great that it is much better ever to seek for it than at any time to find the other kind."

"I," said Trygetius, "shall have to have recourse in my difficulties to my definition. Now, if this seemed faulty to you because it extended to him whom we cannot allow to be a wise man, will you approve, I ask you, if we say that wisdom is *the knowledge of things human and divine, but only of those which have relation to happiness?*"

"That indeed," said the other, "is wisdom, but not that alone. Your former definition trespassed on another's preserve; but this one does not protect its own interests. Hence, the former incurs the charge of greediness, the latter, of folly. I shall myself now explain my view by way of a definition. Wisdom, in my opinion, is *'not only the knowledge of, but also the diligent search for, those things human and divine which have relation to happiness.'* If you wish to split up that definition, the first part, in which knowledge is embraced, pertains to God, and the second part, which is content with searching, pertains to man. God, therefore, is happy in the former. Man is happy in the latter."

"I am amazed," remarked the other, "that your wise man should have to waste his energy as you say."

"How," asked Licentius, "does he waste his energy, when for his expenditure he gains so much? For by the very fact of his seeking, he is wise, and by the fact that he is wise, he is happy. He frees his mind as far as possible from all the folds of the body, and collects himself within himself; [49] he does not allow himself to be torn apart by passions, but in great peace always applies himself to himself, and to God, so that even here in this life he makes full use of reason which, as we have already agreed, constitutes happiness, and finds himself on his last day in this life prepared for the possession of that which he desired, and, having already partaken of human happiness, deservedly enjoys the divine."

CHAPTER 9

Epilogue

24. When Trygetius had for a long time been at a loss as to what he should reply, I said: "I do not think, Licentius, that our friend will be without arguments on this point if we allow him some leisure to find them. Has he at any point been at a loss for a reply? To begin with, when the question was raised about happiness and it was agreed that only the wise man could be happy, since even in the judgment of the foolish, foolishness does not give happiness, he made the point that the wise man ought to be perfect, and that he who was still trying to find out what truth was, was not perfect, and, on that account, was not happy. Then you made difficulties for him by appealing to authority; but he, although he was momentarily put out by the authority of Cicero, nevertheless immediately recovered, and with a certain noble disdain regained at one bound the height of freedom. Once again he seized what had been violently knocked from his hands, by asking you if you thought that he who was still seeking was perfect. If you admitted that he was not perfect, he would have gone back to the beginning and would have tried to demonstrate that by the definition under discussion the man who ruled his life in conformity with the law of his mind was perfect; and from this would result that nobody could be happy unless he were perfect.

"When you had extricated yourself—more deftly than I expected—by maintaining that the perfect man was he who sought for truth with all possible diligence, then, because in fighting your case you exposed yourself by placing too much confidence in that definition of ours, according to which, we were agreed, the happy life, when all was said, was that which was led in conformity to reason, he very definitely put you in a fix again. He overwhelmed your defence and, routed, you would have lost the whole issue, if a truce had not given you respite. For where have the Academics, whose view you defend, concentrated their strength, if not in the definition of error? And if this definition had not come back to your mind during the night, perhaps in a dream, you would have had nothing to reply, although you yourself had already touched upon the very answer you were seeking when you were expounding Cicero's view.

"After that we came to the definition of wisdom, and this you attempted to undermine with such clever subtlety that not even your abettor himself, Albicerius, would perhaps have been wise to your tricks! With what vigilance, with what strength did Trygetius then hold out against you! He had almost tied you up and kept you down, if you had not saved yourself at last with a new definition to the effect that wisdom for man consisted in the search for truth from which, on account of the resulting peace of spirit, happiness would follow. To this point of yours Trygetius need not reply, especially if he asks the favour that for what is left of the day, the discussion be postponed.

25. "But, to be brief, let us now, if you please, close the discussion. Indeed, I think that it is unnecessary for us to delay upon it. We have sufficiently, in view of our purpose, dealt with the matter, one which could be disposed

of in a very few words, if I did not wish to put you through an exercise and make a test of your capacity and tastes. This is a real concern of mine. When I decided to do all I could to encourage you in the quest of truth, I started to ask you how much importance you attached to it. But I found you all so intent on this, that I do not desire more. We desire to be happy, whether that is to be achieved by the finding of, or the diligent search for, truth. Consequently, we must put all other things behind us, if we wish to be happy, and seek out truth.

"And now, let us finish, as I said, this discussion, and, above all, Licentius, let us send a record of it to your father. I have already made him really interested in philosophy. I am only waiting for the good turn of fortune that will admit him to it. He will be better disposed to yearn for these pursuits of ours more ardently when he learns not only by your telling him, but also by reading the record of our debate, that you are thus spending your time with me. But if, as I think, you approve of the Academics, then you must marshal even greater resources to defend them, for I am determined to arraign them myself."

As I said this, luncheon was announced [50] and we broke up the session.

BOOK TWO

THE DOCTRINE OF THE NEW ACADEMY

CHAPTER 1

Exhortation to Romanianus

If it were as inevitable that one should find wisdom when one seeks for it, as it is that one cannot be wise while being without its discipline and knowledge, then straightway the sophistry, obstinacy,[1] inflexibility, or, as I sometimes think, the policy [2] of the Academics which was so appropriate to the times, would have been buried with those times and with the bodies of Carneades and Cicero themselves. But whether because of the many different troubles of this life, which for your own part, Romanianus, you have experienced; or because of a certain stupor or lethargy or sluggishness of our dull minds; or because we despair of finding, since the star of wisdom does not appear as easily to our minds as does the light to our eyes; or, again, because—and this is the common mistake—men, wrongly thinking that they have already found truth, do not seek with diligence, if they do seek, and even acquire an aversion for such search; [3] it comes about that knowledge is possessed seldom and by the few. And so it happens that the weapons of the Academics, when one joins issue with them, seem to be invincible and, as it were, made by Vulcan [4]—and this not to men of little account, but to men

65

of capacity and long training. Accordingly, while one should employ the oars of all available virtues in rowing against those waves and buffetings of fortune, one should especially implore with all devotion and piety the divine help so that the constant application of oneself to noble pursuits of the mind may hold its course, nor be put astray by any chance from reaching the safe and pleasant harbour [5] of philosophy.

This is your first task. I fear the danger involved mostly on your account. From it I want you to be freed. Nor do I cease to pray daily—would that I were worthy enough to be heard!—for favourable winds for you. And it is to the virtue and wisdom [6] itself of the great God that I pray! For what else is He whom the mysteries [7] present to us as the Son of God?

2. Now, you will help me [8] greatly in my prayers for you, if you do not despair of our being heard and strive with us not only with your prayers, but also with your will, and especially with your mind—by nature so elevated—on account of which I seek you, which causes me extraordinary joy, which I ever admire, but which—alas! lies hidden like a thunderbolt in the clouds of family preoccupations. It escapes the notice of many, indeed, of almost everybody. But it cannot escape my notice and that of one or two of your intimates. We have often not only listened carefully to the rumblings of your spirit, but also have seen some of those flashes which announce the thunderbolt. I shall not mention for the moment other instances, but one I shall recall. Who, tell me, ever manifested such sudden power or showed forth such light of mind, as to be able with one groaning of reason and a cer-

tain flame of temperance in one day to overcome completely a passion which had been most fierce the day
before? [9] Will not, then, that power of yours burst forth
someday and turn the mockery of many cynical men into
awe and stupefaction? And will it not first speak on this
earth certain things prophetic of the future, and then cast
off the burden of the whole body and betake itself again
to heaven? [10] Has Augustine said those things of Romanianus in vain? No, He [11] to whom I have given myself completely and whom I now begin to know a little again, will
not allow it!

CHAPTER 2

3. Come with me, then, to philosophy. Here there is
everything that is wont wonderfully to move you whenever you are anxious and hesitating. I have no fears for
you on the score of moral apathy or intellectual laziness.
Who, when there was a moment for relaxation, showed
himself more alert than you in our discussions, or more
penetrating? And shall not I make some return to you for
your favours?

Or is it that I owe you little? When I was but a poor
boy setting out on my studies, you took me up, opening
to me your house, your money, and, what is much more,
your heart. When I lost my father, you comforted me
with your friendship, gave me life with your advice, and
helped me from your resources. In our own town itself
you made me by your patronage, friendship, and the
throwing open of your house to me, almost as distinguished
and important as yourself. When I returned to Carthage

with a view to an advance in my profession, and when I
revealed my hopes and my plan not to any of my family
but to you, although you hesitated a little because of that
deep-seated affection of yours for your own home town—
for I had already begun teaching there—nevertheless,
when you found that you could not overcome a young
man's ambition for what seemed to him to be best for
him, you turned with a measure of benevolence truly
wonderful from opposing my plan to supporting it. You
provided for my venture all that was necessary. Once
again you, who had there looked over, as it were, the cradle
and very nest of my studies, supported me now in my
first efforts when I ventured to fly alone. And even when,
in your absence and without your knowledge, I sailed
away, although you were somewhat hurt with me for not
telling you, as had been my wont, you never brought
yourself to accuse me of arrogance, but remained un-
shaken in your friendship. You made no more of your
children deserted by their teacher than of the integrity of
my inmost heart.

4.   Finally, whatever I now enjoy in my leisure; the fact
that I have escaped from the bonds of needless desires;
that in laying down the burden of deadly anxiety I begin
to breathe again, to recover, to return to myself; [12] that I
seek most seriously for truth; that I am about to discover
it; that I feel confident that I shall arrive at the highest
measure [13] itself—you encouraged me to it, you drove me
on, you made it possible.

Whose [14] agent you were, however, in this, is as yet
conceived by me in faith rather than understood by reason.[15] For when face to face with you I unfolded the secret

fears of my mind, and declared earnestly over and over again that I did not consider any fortune to be good fortune save only that which would give leisure for philosophy, nor any way of life to be happy save only that wherein one lived, so to speak, in philosophy, but that I was held back by the heavy burden of my dependents whose life was supported by my profession, and by many other serious considerations, whether of honour or the embarrassments of family circumstances, you were so overjoyed and inflamed with such a worthy zeal for this way of life, that you said that if you could in any way extricate yourself from the bonds of your importunate lawsuits, you would break all the chains that held me, even going so far as to share your patrimony with me.[16]

5. When, therefore, the flame had been set to us and you went away, we never ceased to yearn after philosophy. Nor did we think of anything else but that life which commended itself to us as both pleasant and suitable. We were, it is true, constant in this thought; yet we were not so keen as we might have been, though we believed that we were keen enough. For since as yet we were untouched by that great fire which was to consume us, we thought that the slow fire with which we burned was the greatest. But lo! when certain books [17] full to the brim, as Celsinus [18] says, had wafted to us good things of Arabia,[19] when they had let a very few [20] drops of most precious unguent fall upon that meagre flame, they stirred up an incredible conflagration—incredible, Romanianus, incredible, and perhaps beyond even what you would believe of me—what more shall I say?—beyond even what I would believe of myself.

What honour, what human pomp, what desire for empty fame,[21] what consolations or attractions of this mortal life could move me then? Swiftly did I begin to return entirely to myself.[22] Actually, all that I did—let me admit it—was to look back from the end of a journey, as it were, to that religion which is implanted in us in our childhood days and bound up in the marrow of our bones. But she indeed was drawing me unknowing to herself. Therefore,[23] stumbling, hastening, yet with hesitation I seized the Apostle Paul. For truly, I say to myself, those men would never have been able to do such great things, nor would they have lived as they evidently did live, if their writings and doctrines were opposed to this so great a good.[24] I read through all of it with the greatest attention and care.[25]

6. And then,[26] indeed, whatever had been the little radiance that had surrounded the face of philosophy before then, she now appeared so great that if I could show it, I do not say to you who have ever burned with the desire for it in the days when it was still unknown to you, but to your adversary [27] himself—and as for him, I do not know whether he is an inspiration to you rather than a hindrance—even he would have contemned and abandoned his Baiaes,[28] his pleasant gardens, his refined and sumptuous feastings, his household troupe, and, finally, whatever now strongly attracts him towards all kinds of pleasures. He would fly, an impassioned and holy lover, amazed and glowing with excitement, to this beauty of philosophy. For even he, we must admit, has a certain beauty of spirit, or rather, the seed of such beauty. It strains to burst forth into true beauty, but puts forth only

twisted and misshapen shoots amidst the filth of vice and the smothering briers of false opinions. All the same, it does continue to bloom, and can be seen, so far as is allowed, by a few who peer carefully and with attention into the thicket. That is why he is so hospitable, so refined in many ways in his banquets, so elegant, so polished, and of such excellent taste and an urbanity that discreetly lends its charms to all things.

CHAPTER 3

7. This is what is commonly called *philocalia*.[29] Do not despise the term because of its common use. For *philocalia* and *philosophia* have almost the same names and wish to be considered, as indeed they are, as being of the same family. What is *philosophia*? Love of wisdom. What is *philocalia*? Love of beauty. The Greeks will tell you so. And what is wisdom? Is it not true beauty itself? These two, then, are sisters, born of the same father. But *philocalia* was dragged down from her heavenly abode by the birdlime of wantonness, and was locked up in an ordinary cage. Nevertheless, the close resemblance of name still belongs to her, a reminder to her captor not to despise her.

Her sister, winging her way unrestrained, frequently takes notice of her in her wingless squalor and poverty, but rarely sets her free; and it is *philosophia* alone that knows from what origin *philocalia* is sprung.

Of this entire allegory—note, I have suddenly become an Aesop!—Licentius will give you a more attractive account in a poem.[30] For indeed, he is almost an accomplished poet. If, then, your adversary, who so loves the false, could with healed and open eyes look upon the true beauty even for a moment, with what delight would he take refuge in the lap of philosophy! How he would there recognize you as a true brother and would embrace you!

You are surprised at what I say, and perhaps laugh at it. But suppose that I could explain it to you, as I would wish; suppose that you could at least hear the voice, though not as yet see the face, of philosophy: you would indeed be surprised; but you would not laugh, nor would you be cynical about your adversary. Believe me, one should never despair of any man, and least of all of men like him. We could cite many precedents. In him you have a kind of bird that easily escapes from its bonds and easily flies back to its home, though many others should remain imprisoned and look on in astonishment.

8. But let me return to ourselves. Let us, as I was saying, Romanianus, devote our attention to philosophy. Let me repay some thanks to you—your son has made a beginning with philosophy. I am putting some restraint on him: I want him to have a careful training in subjects that must be taken before, so that later he may proceed all the more vigorously and firmly. You yourself need not fear that you lack that training. Knowing you as I do, all I wish for you is that you should have a favourable opportunity. Indeed, what can I say about your talents except that I wish they were not as uncommon among men as they are unquestionably present in you? There remain yet two defects and obstacles which hinder a man from finding truth, but on their account I have little fear for you. Yet I am afraid lest you should, because of a too mean opinion of yourself, despair of ever finding truth or,

on the other hand, should believe that you had already
found it. Now, then, if you suffer from the first of these,
perhaps the enclosed discussion will relieve you of it. It
is a fact that you have often been angry with the Academics, and all the more so because you knew so little
about them, and all the more eagerly because you were led
on by your passion for truth. Accordingly, with your patronage to support us, I shall join issue with Alypius and
easily persuade you of my opinion, but only, however, so
as to make it appear probable to you. For you will not
see truth itself, unless you give yourself completely to philosophy. As to the second possibility, namely, that perhaps you assume that you have found some truth, you
were, it is true, already doubting and seeking when you
departed from us; still, if any of the old superstition [31] has
returned to your mind, it will be immediately got rid of
either when I send you a discussion between us concerning
religion [32] or when I discuss many things with you face
to face.

9. I myself am at this time doing nothing but purging
myself of futile and harmful opinions. Accordingly, I
feel that I am better off than you. There is only one thing
of which I envy you, and that is that you should enjoy
alone the company of my Lucilianus.[33] Are you perhaps
jealous in turn that I should say *my* Lucilianus? In saying
so, however, what else have I said but that he belongs to
you and to all of us who are but one? For what shall I ask
you in compensation for missing him? Can I ask for yourself? You know that you owe me that much. But now I
say to both of you: Beware lest you think that you know
anything except that only which you know, as you know

that the sum of one, two, three, and four is ten. But at the same time beware lest you think that by philosophy you will not know truth, or that, at any rate, it cannot be known as clearly as in the instance cited. Believe me, or rather, believe Him who says: *Seek and you shall find.*[34] Knowledge is not to be despaired of. It will be clearer than those numbers.

Now let us come to our theme proper. Too late have I begun to feel that this introduction exceeds its proper measure, and that is no slight fault. For measure is undoubtedly divine,[35] but in my enthusiasm I did not notice my mistake. I shall be more careful, once I am wise!

CHAPTER 4

Summary of Previous Debate

10. After the previous discussion which we have put together in the first book, we held none for almost seven days. We were in the meantime going over the three books of Virgil that follow the first, and studying them, as it seemed to be a suitable occupation at the time. As a result, Licentius became so enthusiastic for poetry, that I felt compelled to restrain him somewhat. For he would not willingly allow himself to be called away to anything else from concentration upon this alone. Nevertheless, when I, so far as I was able, had praised the light of philosophy, he at length consented to take up again the question concerning the Academics which we had postponed.

The day, as it happened, had dawned so bright and clear that we decided that the most suitable thing to do was to brighten [36] up our minds. We got up, therefore, earlier than usual and, because it was urgent, did some work with the farm hands. Then Alypius began: "Before I hear you discussing the Academics, I should like to have read to me the discussion which, you say, took place during my absence. Otherwise, since this present discussion arises from it, I shall be at sea, or at least at a disadvantage in listening to what you have to say."

When this had been done and we realized that we had spent almost the whole morning on it, we decided to return from the fields, where we had been walking, to the house. Then Licentius said to me: "Be good enough, please, to expound briefly for me before lunch the whole Academic position. I do not want to miss anything that would help my side."

"This I shall do," said I, "all the more willingly, because you will eat less while you are thinking of this!"

"Do not be too sure of that!" he replied. "I have often observed that many men, and especially my father, eat the more, the more care-laden they are. And you yourself did not find that when I was thinking over those problems of metre, I neglected the table. Indeed, I am often astonished at myself because of this. Why should one be especially hungry just when one has his mind on something else? Who is it that exerts such power over our hands and teeth when our minds are occupied?"

"Listen rather," I said, "to what you have asked about the Academics, lest, as you reflect upon those problems of measures, I find that you are without measure not only in eating but also in asking questions! If I in the interest of my own side of the argument conceal any point, Alypius will tell you of it."

"We shall have to rely upon your good faith," said Alypius. "For if there were any danger that you might conceal anything, I think that I would find it difficult to catch him out who, as everyone of my friends knows, taught me all those things; and that all the more so as in giving a true account you would be showing yourself interested not in victory, but in accomplishing your real purpose."

CHAPTER 5

Doctrine of the New Academy

11. "I shall," I replied, "play fair, since you have a right to expect it. The Academics, then, insisted on two points: on the one hand, that man could not have knowledge of the things which concerned philosophy, and as for other things, Carneades said that he did not bother about them; and on the other, that, nevertheless, man could be wise and that the whole office of the wise man, as you yourself also, Licentius, explained in our former discussion, was to seek for truth. It follows from this that the wise man will not assent to anything whatever.[37] For if he assented to something uncertain, he must needs fall into error; and for the wise man this is a crime.[38] And not only did they maintain that all things were not certain, but they reinforced their assertion with many arguments.

"As for their opinion that truth could not be perceived, they apparently took this from the famous definition of the Stoic Zeno,[39] who said that that truth could be perceived which was so impressed on the mind from the source of its origin, that it could not originate from whence it did not originate.[40] This can be stated more briefly and plainly in the following way: truth can be perceived by those signs which cannot be present in what is not true. The Academics set about demonstrating with all possible force that such a thing could not possibly be found. Thus, in support of their position great stress was placed upon the want of accord among philosophers,[41] the errors of the senses,[42] dreams and delirium,[43] sophisms and fallacies.[44] And since the same Zeno had also insisted that nothing could be more disgraceful than to indulge in mere opinions, they concluded very cleverly that if nothing could be perceived and mere opinion was disgraceful, the man who was wise would never assent to anything.

12. "They were in consequence of this attacked on all sides. It seemed to follow that he who would not assent to anything, would not do anything.[45] The Academics seemed to picture the wise man, who, they maintained, assented to nothing, as being always asleep and neglectful of his obligations. Accordingly, they put forward their idea of the 'probable,'[46] which they also termed 'what-is-like-truth,' and maintained that the wise man did on no account default in his obligations, since he had something to serve him as a norm of conduct. Truth, however, lies hidden because it is obscured or confused either by some sort of darkness inherent in nature, or by the misleading resemblance that things have to each other.[47] At the same time, they said, the very refraining from, or, so to speak, suspending, assent, was a wholly significant action in the wise man.[48]

"I think that I have, as you wished, briefly explained the whole matter, and have not departed, Alypius, from your injunction; that is, I acted, as it is said, in good faith. For if I have not described something just as it is, or omitted something, I have done nothing such deliberately. My own conscience satisfies me that I have presented this in good faith. Obviously, a man who is in error requires instruction, but he who is deceitful must be recognized as one to be guarded against. The first demands a good teacher, the second, a disciple who is on his guard."

13.   Then Alypius said: "I thank you for having satisfied Licentius and relieved me of a burden. For you had no more reason to fear that you should omit something in order to test me—for why else should you do so?—than I that I should have to expose you on some point or other. Now, if it is not too wearisome a task for you, I wish you would explain—not to supply anything that is wanting in your treatment of our inquiry, but to supply information that the inquirer lacks: what is the difference between the New Academy and the Old?"

"I confess," I said, "it is quite wearisome. You will do me a favour if you will let me keep to myself for a moment, while you distinguish between those names and expound the position of the New Academy. I must admit, of course, that the point you have raised is of the greatest relevance."

"I had almost believed," he replied, "that you wanted to keep me also from lunch, if I did not already suspect that you were more upset by Licentius, and if his demand had not required of us that whatever complication there is in this question should be explained to him before lunch."

He was about to complete his remarks, when my mother [49]—for we had meanwhile arrived at the house—began to hustle us to our lunch so that we had no opportunity for discussion.

CHAPTER 6

The Position of the New Academy

14. Afterwards, when we had eaten as much as was necessary to satisfy our hunger, we returned to the meadow, and Alypius began: "I shall do as you wish, nor should I care to refuse. If I omit nothing in my account, the compliment will be to your teaching and to my memory as well. But if, perhaps, I make a mistake in any point, you will make good the deficiency, so that in future I may not fear these commissions.

"It is my opinion that the breaking off of the New Academy did not come about so much from opposition to the old teaching as from opposition to the Stoics.[50] Nor indeed ought it to be called a breaking away. The new question raised by Zeno had to be discussed and resolved. For the point about non-perception, although it had not provoked any conflicts then, nevertheless can reasonably be thought to have been present to the minds of the Old Academy. One can, moreover, easily prove this by the authority of Socrates himself, and Plato and others of the old persuasion. These men believed that they could shield themselves from error so long as they were careful about committing themselves to an assent.[51] They did not, however, introduce into their schools any special discussion on this topic, nor indeed did they clearly precise the question as to whether or no truth could be perceived. But Zeno brought this forward as something new and unexplored, contending that nothing could be perceived unless it was so manifestly true that it could be distinguished from what was not true through a dissimilarity in indications, and that the wise man must not admit an opinion.[52] Arcesilas,[53] when he heard this, denied that any such truth was available to man, and insisted that the life of the wise man must not be exposed to the hazard of such opinion either. Accordingly, he went so far as to conclude that one should not assent to anything.

15. "This was the position, then, namely, that the Academy had been developed rather than suffered attack. But a disciple of Philo,[54] Antiochus,[55] a man whom some adjudged to be more interested in reputation than truth, arose and brought into conflict the teaching of both Academies. He declared that the New Academics had attempted to introduce something that was new and quite removed from the doctrine of the old school. He appealed to the testimony of the physicists of old, and of other great philosophers to prove his point, and attacked the New Academics themselves on the ground that, although they admitted that they did not know truth itself, they yet maintained that they were following 'what-was-like-truth.' He collected many arguments which I do not propose to expound to you now. One point, however, he maintained above all others: the wise man could perceive truth.

"This is my view of the conflict between the New and the Old Academy. If that conflict is not as I have described it, I would request you to give an exhaustive account of it to Licentius for both of us. But if it is as I have tried to say, proceed with the discussion which you have undertaken."

CHAPTER 7

Probability and Verisimilitude

16. Then I said: "Why, Licentius, have you been silent
so long during the course of these unexpectedly lengthy
remarks? Now do you know what your Academics are?"

He smiled modestly, and was a little upset by my chal-
lenge. "I regret," he replied, "having maintained so
strongly against Trygetius that happiness depended upon
the search for truth. Indeed, your question embarrasses
me so that I am scarcely anything but wretched. At any
rate, if you have any feeling in you, my case must seem
pitiable to you. But why should I be foolish enough to tor-
ment myself? Or why should I be daunted when I am supported by a cause so excellent? No, indeed, I shall not give
in to anything but the truth."

"Do you approve, then," I asked, "of the New Academy?"

"Most certainly," he replied.

"Therefore, they seem to you to maintain the truth?"

He was about to give his assent when, warned by a
chuckle from Alypius, he hesitated for a second, and then
said: "Repeat that little question."

I said, "Do the Academics seem to you to maintain the
truth?"

Again he was silent for a long time. "I do not know if
it is the truth," he replied, "but, at any rate, it is probable,
and I cannot see anything else that I can follow."

"You know," I asked, "that they themselves describe the probable also as 'what-is-like-truth'?"

"Yes," he replied.

"Therefore," I said, "the teaching of the Academics is 'what-is-like-truth.' "

"Yes," he said.

"I beg you," said I, "give me your best attention. If a man who never saw your father himself, yet, on seeing your brother, asserted that he was like your father, would you not think that he was mentally affected or talking at random?"

He was silent for a long time. Then he replied: "No, I do not think that is absurd."

17. When I began to reply, he said: "Wait a moment, please." Then, with a smile, he said, "Tell me, are you already certain that you will win the argument?"

"Suppose that I am," I replied. "You ought not, all the same, on that account abandon your cause, especially since this discussion between us has been undertaken to train you and to incite you to cultivate your mind."

"But have I," he returned, "either read the writings of the Academics,[56] or have I been instructed in as varied knowledge as you, who come thus prepared against me?"

I replied: "Neither had those who first defended your case read the Academics. And if training and a storehouse of knowledge is wanting to you, your capacity should not be so deplorably weak that, without my making any attack on you, you yield to a few remarks and questions of mine. To be sure, I am already beginning to fear that Alypius may take your place sooner than I wish. I shall not be proceeding so unconcernedly, if he is my adversary."

"Well," said he, "I wish I were already beaten in the argument. Then I could for once listen to you arguing and, what is more, I could see you at it. This is a sight which I would enjoy more than anything else. Obviously, since you have decided to gather up your words rather than waste them, to catch them as they come from your lips with the pen and not allow them, as they say, to fall to the ground, one will also be able to read what you have to say. But somehow or other, when the principals themselves who engage in the discussion are present to one's eyes, a good debate, though the practical value of it may not be enhanced, nevertheless, certainly gives greater pleasure."

18. "We thank you," I replied. "But these sudden delights of yours have led you to make the rash statement that nothing could give you more pleasure than to see us as we discussed. But if you saw your father, than whom certainly no one will drink of philosophy with greater passion after so long a thirst, discussing and talking of those things with us, while I would think myself happier than ever before, what, I ask you, should you rightly think and say?"

Here Licentius cried a little. When he was able to speak, he raised his hands and looked up to heaven: "And when, O God," said he, "shall I see this? But no, there is nothing we need despair of obtaining from Thee."

Almost all of us were distracted from the discussion and began to cry.[57] I struggled with myself and with difficulty regained my composure. "Come," I said, "gather your forces again. I had told you long before to collect them wherever you could, since you were to be the defender of the Academics. I cannot suppose that already,

Even before the trumpet sounds, fear grips your limbs,[58]

or that you wish to be taken prisoner so soon in order to look on at another's fighting."

At this point Trygetius, when he had decided that we were sufficiently composed again, said: "You, who are so dear to God, Licentius, may well hope that He will grant your prayer before you offer it! Have faith! Indeed, you who cannot find an answer to an argument, and yet say that you wish to be vanquished, seem to me to be of little faith."

We laughed. Then Licentius said: "Let you speak, then, you who find happiness not in discovering the truth, and certainly still less in looking for it."

19. We all felt more cheerful because of the good humour of the young men, and to Licentius I said: "Pay attention to my question, and, if you can, return with renewed confidence and vigour to where we left off."

"I am ready," he said, "as far as I can be. Now, then, if the man who saw my brother had known from hearsay that my brother was like my father, can he be taken to be mentally affected or talking at random for believing the report?"

"Could not he," said I, "at least be called foolish?"

"Not necessarily," he replied, "unless he insists that he *knows* this to be so. Obviously, if he follows as *probable* that which is frequently reported, he cannot be convicted of any rashness whatsoever."

Then I said: "Let us consider the matter precisely for a moment, and as it were, place it before our eyes. Suppose that this someone of whom we are talking, were here with us. Along comes your brother. The man asks: 'Whose son is this?' The answer is given: 'The son of a certain Romanianus.' The other remarks: 'How like his father he is! How right was the report I heard!' You or someone else interjects: 'My good man, so you know Romanianus?' 'No,' he says. 'All the same, he seems to me to be like him.' Would anyone be able to keep from laughing?"

"Of course not," he replied.

"Therefore," I said, "you see what follows."

"I have seen it this long time," he replied. "But I would like to hear the conclusion which we are coming to, from your own lips. You know that you should start to feed him whom you have taken prisoner!"

"Well, I shall draw the conclusion," I said. "It is obvious that in the same way are your Academics to be laughed at, since they say that in practical matters they follow 'what-is-like-truth,' although actually they do not know what truth itself is."

CHAPTER 8

20.   Then Trygetius remarked: "The precaution taken by the Academics seems to me to be very different from the drivelling of the fellow you talk of. For they arrive by reason at 'what-is-like-truth,' while that fool of yours was guided by report, which is the worst possible authority."

I rejoined: "As though he were not a still greater fool if he said: 'True, I have no knowledge whatever of his father, nor do I know by report how like his father he is. Just the same, he seems to me to be like him'!"

"Yes, certainly," he replied, "he would be a greater fool. But what is the point?"

"In the same class with him belong those who say: 'We do not, indeed, know truth, but that which we see is like that which we do not know.'"

"'Probable' is the term they use," he said.

I asked: "Why do you insist on using that term? Do you deny that they call it 'what-is-like-truth'?"

He retorted: "I deliberately used the term in order to exclude the element of 'likeness.' For it seemed to me that the idea of 'report' has wrongly obtruded itself upon the question as you put it. The Academics do not trust even in human eyes, to say nothing of the thousand—as the poets picture them—fantastic eyes of report." [59]

"But who am I that I should defend the Academics? Or do you envy me my freedom from the discussion? Here is Alypius. His coming will, I hope, set us free. You, we are inclined to think, have been afraid of him all along—and not without reason."

21. In the ensuing silence both fixed their eyes on Alypius, who began: "Indeed, I would like, as best I could, to give your side some little assistance. But the omen you give frightens me. Unless, however, my hope deceives me, it will be easy for me to banish this fear. You see, I am encouraged at once by the knowledge that he who is now attacking the Academics almost stole the part of Trygetius when he was beaten, and now by your own avowal, it is probable that Trygetius' side will win. The other thing I fear more, namely, that I should incur the charge of negligence in deserting my own function, and of forwardness in assuming that of another. You remember, I take it, that

I was appointed arbiter of the discussion."

"That is one thing," said Trygetius, "but this is another. We beg you to permit yourself for once to be just an ordinary individual in the discussion."

"I must not refuse," he said, "lest in seeking to avoid both forwardness and negligence I fall into the snare of pride—which is the most heinous of all vices—in seeking to retain longer than you allow an honour which you have given me."

CHAPTER 9

22. "Well, then, my accuser of the Academics, be good enough to tell us your mission, that is to say, whom are you defending in attacking them? I am actually afraid that in refuting the Academics you may wish to show that you are an Academic yourself!"

I replied: "You know well, I think, that there are two types of accusers. Even if Cicero in his modesty said that he was an accuser of Verres only in so far as he was a defender of the Sicilians,[60] it does not necessarily follow that he who accuses someone is defending someone else."

Alypius rejoined: "Have you at least a good basis on which your opinion is founded?"

"It is easy," I replied, "to answer that question, especially for me to whom it does not come suddenly. I have gone through the whole thing for myself and I have pondered it much and for a long time. Accordingly, Alypius, listen to what, as I think, you already know well. I do not want this discussion to be undertaken merely for the sake of discussing. Let us have done with these preliminary exercises in which we joined with these young people [61] and in which philosophy, so to say, was ready to jest with us. Let us, therefore, put away from us children's tales! We are concerned with life,[62] with morality, with the spirit—that spirit which hopes to overcome the antagonism of every kind of illusion, and, possessing itself of truth, to return in triumph over the passions to that region, so to speak, from which it sprung, and, having thus received temperance as a bride, to reign, safer in its return to heaven.[63] You understand what I say. Again, let us discard all those trifling things!

Weapons must be forged for a doughty warrior! [64]

"But there is nothing that I have ever desired less than that among such as have lived and conversed together a great deal, anything should occur from which, as it were, fresh conflicts might arise. I have decided, however, to commit to writing now those points which we have often gone over together both to help the memory, which is an untrustworthy guardian of what one has thought out, and so as to induce those young men to apply themselves to these problems and attempt to approach and deal with them for themselves.

23. "Accordingly, how can it be that you do not know that up to now I have arrived at no certainty, but have been impeded in the search by the arguments and disputes of the Academics? Somehow or other they persuaded me of the probability—to keep to their term for the moment— that man cannot find truth. Consequently, I became lazy and very slothful, nor did I have the courage to seek for what clever and learned men [65] were not permitted to find. Unless, therefore, I shall persuade myself to the same ex-

tent that truth can be found, as the Academics persuade themselves that it cannot, I shall not dare to seek for it, nor have I anything to defend. Wherefore, please withdraw your question.

"Let us rather discuss among ourselves as closely as possible, the question whether or no truth can be found. For my part, I think I can even now advance many arguments against the Academic position. Between them and me there is this one difference: they think it probable that truth cannot be found, and I, that it can. If they are but pretending,[66] then ignorance of truth is peculiar to me only, but it is more likely to be common to us both."

CHAPTER 10

24. "Now," said Alypius, "I can proceed confidently. I see that you will be not so much an opponent as a helper. Accordingly, so as to avoid wandering in the argument, let us, I ask you, first make sure that in dealing with this question in which I appear to have succeeded to your defeated adversaries, we do not go off into mere verbal controversy. By your own suggestion and on the authority of Tullius we have often insisted that that was a bad thing.[67] Unless I am mistaken, then, Licentius first said that he approved of the Academic 'probable,' and then you asked him if he was aware that the 'probable' was also called by them 'what-is-like-truth.' He stated clearly that it was so. And I know well, since it is from you that I myself learned them, that you know the doctrines of the Academics. Therefore, since you have them well impressed

upon your mind, as I said, I cannot understand why you should cavil about words."

I replied: "This is not, I assure you, a dispute about words, but, rather, a serious dispute about serious issues. I do not think that the Academics were the kind of men who did not know how to give a thing its proper name. On the contrary, they seem to me to have chosen these terms both at once to conceal from the unintelligent and reveal to the more alert,[68] their real opinion. Why I think this and how I understand it, I shall explain when I have discussed first the points which, as men think, they, as the apparent enemies of human knowledge, advance.

"I am, then, very glad that we have got so far in our debate to-day, for now we are agreed about, and are aware of, what is at issue between us. Certainly, the Academics seem to me to have been quite serious and foreseeing. If there is anything that we shall attack now, it will be those who have said that the Academics opposed the finding of truth. And do not think that I am afraid: I shall be quite willing to arm myself against the Academics, too, if they really stood by what we read in their books,[69] and did not advance it merely so as to conceal their true opinion, lest certain sacred truths should be betrayed rashly by them to minds defiled, and, so to speak, profane. This I would do to-day, but that the setting of the sun already forces us to return to the house."

Thus far our discussion took us on that day.

CHAPTER 11

The "Probable"

25. Though the following day dawned no less pleasant and peaceful, we could scarcely get away from domestic preoccupations. The greater part of it had already passed, especially in the writing of letters, when, with barely two hours remaining, we went to the meadow. The weather was really unusually fair and inviting, and we decided that we should not allow even the little time that was left, to be wasted. When, therefore, we had come to the tree where we usually sat, and had settled down, I said: "I would like you young men, since we are not to embark on anything serious to-day, to rehearse for me how Alypius yesterday answered the little question that upset you."

To this Licentius remarked: "It is so short that it takes no effort to recall it; but as for its being an easy question, that is for you to demonstrate. Indeed, as far as I can see, once the matter at issue had been clarified, it did not allow you to raise a dispute about words."

"Have you all," I said, "sufficiently appreciated the point and force of this?"

"Yes, I think I have," said Licentius. "But please explain it a little. I have indeed often heard you say that it is a disgrace for disputants to haggle about words, when no difference about the subject matter remains; but this is too fine a point that I should be asked to explain it."

26. "Listen then," I said, "to what is meant. The Aca-

demics· call that the 'probable' or 'what-is-like-truth' which can induce us to act while we withhold our assent. I say 'while we withhold assent,' inasmuch as we do not judge that what we do is true, or think that we know it, but we do it all the same. As for example, if a man were to ask us if, since last night was so bright and clear, today's sun would rise with the same cheerful mien, I think we would say that we did not know, but that we thought so. 'The things, then,' says the Academic, 'that I have decided to describe as "probable" or "what-is-like-truth," are all of such kind. If you wish to call them by another name, I make no objection. I am quite satisfied if you have grasped well what I mean, that is to say, what things I have in mind in using these terms: the wise man should not be an artificer of words, but an inquirer into realities.' [70] Do you now grasp fully how those silly toys, with which I was trying to arouse your interest, have been dashed from my hands?"

When both replied that they had understood, and kept looking at me in anticipation of what I would reply to them, I said: "What do you think? Was Cicero, whose words I have just quoted, so poor a Latinist that he used unsuitable terms for the things he had in mind?"

CHAPTER 12

27. To this Trygetius replied: "Indeed, since the matter is obvious, we do not think that we should provoke any dispute about words. So, think rather of what you will reply to Alypius who has relieved us, but whom now you want to attack again."

"A moment, please," Licentius said in turn, "something
is dawning upon me. I am beginning to see that that
argument of yours should not so easily have been disposed
of." He was silent for a while, lost in thought. Then he
said: "Nothing, I submit, seems more absurd than that a
man who does not know what truth is, should say that he
follows 'what-is-like-truth.' Nor does that comparison of
yours disconcert me. For if I were asked if, judging by the
evening sky, there will be no rain on the morrow, I am
right in replying that it does not seem likely. I do in fact
know some truth. I know, for instance, that this tree cannot at a moment's notice turn into silver; and many other
facts like this I can truly say that I know without being
over-confident, and I note that like these are those things
which I call 'what-is-like-truth.' But you, Carneades, or any
other Greek pest, to say nothing of our own brood—for
why should I hesitate to desert to the side of him whose
captive I am by right of victory?—you, I say, whence do
you get this 'what-is-like-truth,' since you say that you
know no truth whatever? 'But I could not get another
name for it,' says Carneades. Why, then, do we bother to
discuss anything with one who does not even know how to
express himself?"

28. "I am not a man," said Alypius, "who fears de-
serters. Much less so the great Carneades. I do not know
whether it is through boyish or youthful levity that you
judged it proper to assail him with insults rather than
with some weapon. But in support of his teaching, whose
point of departure was always the probable, this will be
quite sufficient to silence you for the present, the fact,
namely, that we are so far removed from the discovery of

truth that you yourself can be instanced as a telling argument against yourself.[71] By one little question you were so shaken in your position that you were at a complete loss as to where you should stand. But let us postpone this and your knowledge, which you have just avowed was communicated to you regarding this tree, to another time. For, although you have now chosen another side, nevertheless I shall take pains to explain to you what I said shortly before. We had not got as far, I think, as the question as to whether or no truth could be found; I was of the opinion, however, that this at least should be decided right at the threshold of my defence—a point where I had seen you prostrate and exhausted—namely, whether one should not seek 'what-is-like-truth,' or the 'probable,' or whatever else it can be called, which the Academics hold to be enough. It is of no interest to me if you seem to yourself to be even now an excellent discoverer of truth. Afterwards, if you are thankful for my coming to your rescue now, you may, perhaps, teach me what you know."

CHAPTER 13

What was the Real Teaching of the New Academy?

29. Here I intervened because Licentius, his face flushed with shame, was cowed by the onset of Alypius: "Alypius, you have preferred to speak in every way but the way we ought to when we engage in debate with these boys who do not know how to speak."

Alypius replied: "Since I as well as everybody else have known for a long time, and now by your own profession you give evidence enough of the same, namely, that you are an expert in speaking, I wish you would first explain the use of this investigation of yours. It is either irrelevant, as I think, and it would be much more irrelevant to reply to it; or, if you decide that it is to the point, in which case it is too difficult for me to explain, then heed my earnest plea: do not weary of being my teacher."

"You remember," I said, "that I promised yesterday to treat of those words later. And now yonder sun reminds me to put away again in their boxes the toys which I set before the boys—especially since I take them out for the sake of ornament rather than to sell them. But before darkness, ever the advocate of the Academics, prevents writing, I would like it to be fully agreed between us to-day as to what question we shall attack the first thing in the morning. Accordingly, tell me, please, do you think that the Academics had a definite teaching about truth and were opposed to imparting it indiscriminately to minds ignorant or uncleansed, or that their thoughts were really at one with the tenor of their disputations?"

30. He replied: "I shall not rashly assert what their mind on the matter was. In so far as one can gather this from their books, you know better what words they are accustomed to use for the expression of their opinion. If you ask me what I think myself, I reply that I think that truth has not yet been discovered. I add, too—a point on which you were questioning me in connection with the Academics—that I think that it cannot be found, not only because of my ingrained conviction which you have observed in me practically from the start, but also on the authority of great and outstanding philosophers, to whose

opinions we are somehow induced to submit, whether through our own mental impotence, or because of the keenness of their minds, which, we are forced to believe, cannot possibly be surpassed."

"This is exactly what I wanted," I said. "I was afraid lest if we should see eye to eye, our debate would be a stunted affair; for there would be nobody who would compel us to treat the matter from the other side so that it might be thrashed out by us as well as we can.[72] Therefore, in case this had happened, I was prepared to ask you to defend the Academics on the lines that, in your opinion, they not only argued that truth could not be discovered, but also that they were convinced of this.

The point, therefore, at issue between us is whether or no their arguments make it probable that nothing can be perceived and that one should not assent to anything. If you demonstrate that they do this, I shall gladly yield. But if I can demonstrate that it is much more probable both that the wise man can arrive at truth, and that one should not always withhold one's assent, you will have no excuse, I think, for refusing to come over to my side."

He and all that were present agreed to this, and as the shadows of evening were already falling about us, we returned to the house.

BOOK THREE

WISDOM AND KNOWLEDGE

CHAPTER 1

Man's Need of Truth

When on the day following that on which we had
finished the discussion contained in the second book, we
had taken our places in the baths—for the day was too dis-
agreeable to go to the meadow—I began as follows: "I take
it that you all have noted well the points which we have
decided to take in the problem that we are discussing. But
before I take up my own role, which is to explain those
points, I would like you to show your good will and listen
to a few remarks not irrelevant to our subject—remarks
which have to do with our hopes, our life, and our principles. It is our business, neither trivial nor unnecessary, but
rather, in my opinion, most necessary and of the greatest
importance, to seek with all our strength for truth. Alypius
and myself are in agreement about this. For all philosophers believed that the wise man, as they conceived him,
had found truth; but the Academics declared that their
wise man must try with his utmost efforts to find it, and
that in fact he does so conscientiously, except that, since
truth is either hidden in obscurity or because of confusion does not stand out clearly, he follows as a guide in
action that which seems to him to be probable and 'like-
the-truth.'

"The same conclusion was reached in your own recent

discussion. Thus one of you contended that happiness for man lay in the finding of truth, and the other was satisfied that merely seeking for truth constituted happiness. Accordingly, none of us has any doubt that we should attend to the seeking of truth above everything else. Let us consider, then, how, for example, we may judge ourselves to have spent yesterday. Of course, you were free to give your time to your studies. For instance, you, Trygetius, spent the time pleasantly reading the poems of Virgil, and Licentius applied himself to poetic composition, to which he is so much given that it was especially for his sake that I decided to bring up this topic. It is high time that philosophy should take and hold a greater part in his mind than poetry or any other subject.

CHAPTER 2

Is Man Independent of Fortune?

2. "But, tell me, did you not feel sorry for us? We had gone to bed on the previous evening with the intention of dealing with practically nothing else but our postponed discussion when we should arise. The urgency, however, of matters that had to be taken care of about the place was such, that we were completely taken up by them and we had barely two hours at the close of day in which to give ourselves time to breathe. Hence, it has always been my opinion that, whilst the *wise* man indeed needs nothing, he needs much help from fortune to *become* wise.[1] But perhaps Alypius holds a different view."

Alypius replied: "I do not know as yet what you think

to be the province of fortune. If you believe that fortune's help is necessary for the contemning of fortune herself, then I am with you in that belief. But if you believe that it is her function to provide only those bodily necessities which cannot be had without her favour, then I do not agree. For either the man who does not yet possess wisdom, but is desirous of it, can procure the things we deem necessary for life, even if fortune be adverse and unwilling, or we must admit that she dominates the whole life of the wise man—since the wise man himself, too, cannot dispense with the need of bodily necessities."

3. "You say, then," I replied, "that he who is seeking wisdom needs fortune, but you deny that this is so for the wise man?"

"To say the same thing over again has its advantages," he said, "so I in turn ask you if you think that fortune helps towards the contemning of herself. If you think so, then I do say that he who seeks wisdom is in great need of assistance from fortune."

"I do think so," I answered. "It is by her help that he becomes such as can contemn her. And this is not absurd: when we are infants we need a mother's breasts, and by them it is brought about that later on we can live and be strong without them."

"It is clear to me," he said, "that if there is no disagreement in our minds in conceiving them, our opinions agree; though a person might think that he should argue the point that it is not breasts or fortune, but some other thing that helps us to contemn fortune or breasts."

"It is a simple matter," I said, "to give another comparison. For instance, a man cannot cross the Aegean, even if he wants only to get to the other side, without a ship or some other means of transport, or, so that I might not seem to avoid mention of the method evolved by Daedalus [2] himself, some device constructed for this purpose, or some preternatural power. When he has made the crossing, he is ready to throw away and contemn whatever brought him across.[3] So, too, whoever wishes to arrive at the safe and tranquil land and haven of wisdom, seems to me to have fortune's help in his purpose. I shall give but one example of what I mean: he cannot be wise, if he be blind and deaf; and blindness and deafness are in the power of fortune. Once he has achieved this purpose, though he should be considered to be still in need of certain things pertaining to the health of his body, it is evident, nevertheless, that such things are not necessary so that he be wise, but only that he should continue to exist among men."

"Nay, more," said Alypius, "if he be blind and deaf, he will, in my opinion, rightly contemn the acquisition of wisdom and that life itself, for which wisdom is sought."

4. "Nevertheless," I said, "since life itself during our days on earth is in the power of fortune, and only a living person can become wise, must we not admit that we need her favour in order to reach wisdom?"

"But," he replied, "since wisdom is necessary to those only who are alive, and if life be taken away no need for wisdom remains, I do not fear fortune as far as the continuation of life is concerned. For it is because I live that I desire wisdom, and it is not because I desire wisdom that I wish to live. If fortune, then, takes my life away, she takes away the reason for my seeking wisdom. There is no reason, therefore, why I should either desire the favour, or fear the interference of fortune in becoming wise. But perhaps you have other considerations to offer."

I asked: "You do not think, then, that he who is seeking for wisdom can be prevented by fortune from becoming wise, if one suppose that she does not deprive him of his life?"

"No, I do not," he replied.

CHAPTER 3

The Difference between the Wise Man and the Philosopher

5. "I would like you," I said, " to tell me briefly what you think to be the difference between the wise man and the philosopher."

"In my opinion," he said, "the wise man differs in no way from the philosopher except that the wise man in a certain way possesses [4] those things which can only be longed for—however eagerly—by the philosopher."

"Now, then," I asked, "what are these things? For my part, I see no difference except that one knows wisdom, and the other wants to know."

"If," he said, "you give us a simple definition of knowledge, your point already becomes more clear."

"No matter how I define it," I replied, "all are agreed that there cannot be knowledge of what is not true."

"In my remark," he said, "I purposed to limit that question for you, in order to prevent an unconsidered concession of mine from allowing your oratory to gallop unrestrained over the plains of this cardinal question." [5]

I replied: "To be sure, you have left me no galloping space at all! Indeed, if I mistake not, we have arrived at that for which I have been striving all the time—the end. For if, as you stated so acutely and truly, there is no difference between the philosopher and the wise man except that the former loves, the latter possesses, wisdom—for which reason you did not hesitate to use the term proper here, 'possession'; and since no one can possess wisdom in his mind, if he has not learned anything; and since no one can learn anything, if he does not know anything; and since no one can know what is not true: therefore, the wise man knows truth, for you yourself have just admitted that he has wisdom, that is to say, its 'possession,' in his mind."

"I may," he said, "seem to be impertinent, but I do wish to deny that I admitted that the wise man has the 'possession' of the power of inquiring into divine and human things. I do not see why you should think that it is not the 'possession' of discovered probabilities that he has."

"Do you concede to me," I asked, "that no one knows what is not true?"

"Certainly," he replied.

"Assert, if you can," I said, "that the wise man does not know wisdom."

"But why," said he, "do you in this way restrict the whole question? Could he not believe that he has grasped wisdom?"

"Give me your hand," I said, "If you recall, this is the point which I said yesterday that I would prove; and now I am happy that it was not I who expressed this conclusion, but that you offered it to me spontaneously on your own. For I said that between the Academics and myself there was this difference, that while they thought it probable that truth could not be perceived, I believed that, though I myself had not yet found it, it could be found by the wise man. You now, when pressed by my question as to whether or no the wise man did not know wisdom, reply: 'He thinks that he knows.' "

"Well," he asked, "what follows from that?"

"This," I replied, "that if he thinks that he knows wisdom, he does not think that the wise man cannot know anything. Or, if wisdom is nothing, then say so."

6. "I should indeed believe," he replied, "that we had arrived at our final objective, but that suddenly, as we joined hands, I realized that we are very far apart and separated by a long distance. For, obviously, the only point at issue between us was, whether or no the wise man could arrive at the perception of truth. You asserted that he could. I denied it. But I do not think that I have now conceded to you anything except that the wise man can believe that he has achieved the wisdom of probabilities. That wisdom I understood to be concerned with the investigation of things human and divine. We are, I take it, agreed on that."

"You will not," I said, "evolve a method of escape by involving the issue! For the moment, it would seem to me, you are arguing merely to try your skill. You know well that these young men can scarcely as yet follow subtle and acute reasoning. You abuse, then, the ignorance of your jury. It is a case of your saying as much as you like simply because no one will protest. Now, a few moments ago, when I was questioning you as to whether or no the wise man knew wisdom, you said that he believed that he knew.

But he who believes that the wise man knows wisdom, certainly cannot believe that the wise man knows nothing. Such a proposition is impossible, unless a man dares to say that wisdom is nothing. From this it follows that in this your view is identical with mine. For my view that the wise man knows something, is, I believe, also yours, since you believe that the wise man believes that he knows wisdom."

He replied: "I think that you wish to exercise your powers just as much as I do. I am surprised at that, for you have no need of any practice in this matter at all. I may, of course, still be blind in seeing a difference between 'believing-one-knows' and 'knowing,' and between the wisdom bound up with investigation, and truth itself. I do not see how these opinions expressed by each of us can be squared with one another."

As we were being called to lunch, I said: "I am not displeased that you should be so obstinate. Either both of us do not know what we are talking about, and we must, therefore, take steps to avoid such a disgrace; or this is true of only one of us, and to leave him so and neglect him, is equally disgraceful. We shall, however, have to meet again in the afternoon; for, just when I thought that we had finished, you began to indulge in fisticuffs with me."

They all laughed at this and we departed.

CHAPTER 4

The Wise Man Knows Truth

7.   When we returned, we found Licentius, whose thirst for Helicon [6] could never be quenched, eagerly trying to think out verses. For he had quietly arisen without having had anything to drink, in the middle of lunch, even though this was over almost as quickly as it had begun. I remarked to him: "I certainly hope that some day you will realize your heart's desire and master poetry. Not that I take such pleasure in the art; but I see that you are so obsessed by it that you cannot escape from this infatuation except through tiring of it, and this is a common experience when one has reached perfection. And another thing, since you have a good voice, I would prefer that you would ply our ears with your verses than that you should sing, like poor little birds that we see in cages, from those Greek tragedies words which you do not understand. But I suggest that you go, if you wish, and drink something and then return to our school, provided the *Hortensius* and philosophy still mean something to you. To her you have already dedicated the tender first fruits of your mind in your recent discussion—a discussion which inflamed you even more than does poetry for the knowledge of great and truly fruitful things. But while I endeavour to bring you back to the circle of those studies by which the mind is developed, I fear lest it become a labyrinth to you, and I almost repent of having held you back from your first impulse."

Licentius blushed and went away to drink. He was very

thirsty. Moreover, he could thus avoid me, who seemed likely to have more and sharper things to say to him.

8.   When he had come back, I began as follows, while all paid close attention: "Alypius, can it be that we disagree on a matter which to me seems really very evident?"

"It is not surprising," he said, "if what you say is manifest to you should be obscure to me. After all, many things evident enough in themselves can be more evident to some than to others; so, too, some things obscure in themselves can be still more obscure to some people. For, believe me, that if this matter is evident to you, there is some one else to whom it is even more evident, and still another person to whom it is more obscure than it is to me. But I beg you to make what is evident still more evident, so that you may cease to regard me as a diehard in argument."

"Please, listen closely," I said, "and do not bother for the moment to reply to my question. Knowing you and myself well, I feel that with a little attention my point will become clear and one of us will quickly convince the other. Now, then, did you not say—or, perhaps, I did not hear rightly—that the wise man thought that he knew wisdom?"

He said that this was so.

"Let us," I said, "forget about the wise man for the moment. Are you yourself wise or are you not?"

"I am anything but that," he replied.

"But," said I, "do give me your own personal opinion about the Academic wise man. Do you think that he knows wisdom?"

He replied: "Is thinking that one knows the same as, or

different from, knowing? I am afraid lest confusion on this point might afford cover to either of us."

9. "This," I said, "has become what they call a Tuscan argument: for this is the name they gave to an argument when instead of answering a difficulty, a man proposes another. It was this that our poet—let us win the attention of Licentius for a moment—in his *Eclogues* judged fairly to be rustic and downright countryish: when one asks the other, where the heavens are no more than three ells broad, the other replies:

In what lands do flowers grow engraved with the names of kings? [7]

Please, Alypius, do not think that we can allow ourselves that merely because we are on the farm! At least, let these little baths [8] serve you as a reminder of the decorum that is expected in places of learning. Kindly answer my question: Do you think that the Academic wise man knows wisdom?"

"Not to lose ourselves," he replied, "parrying words with words—I think that he thinks that he knows wisdom."

"Therefore," I said, "you think that he does not know wisdom? I am not asking you what you think the wise man thinks, but if you think that the wise man knows wisdom. You can, I take it, say either yes or no, here and now."

"I do wish," he returned, "that the matter were either as easy for me as it is for you, or as difficult for you as it is for me; and that you were not so insistent, and put such great store in these points. For, when you asked me what I thought about the Academic wise man, I replied that in my opinion it seemed to him that he knew wisdom: I did not wish to assent rashly that I knew, or, what would be just as rash, say that he knew."

"I shall be greatly obliged," I said, "if you will be good enough, first, to answer the question I put to you, and not those that you yourself put to yourself. Secondly, you may disregard for the moment what satisfaction I expect to receive from this: I know that you are as interested in it as in your own expectations. Obviously, if I deceive myself by this line of questioning, I shall promptly come over to your side and we shall finish the dispute. Finally, banish the anxiety which I note is somehow gripping you, and pay close attention, so that you will have no trouble in understanding what I want you to reply.

"Now, you said that you did not give your assent or denial—but this is just what you should do with my question—for the reason that you did not wish to state rashly that you knew what you did not know. As if I were to ask you what you know, and not what you think! And now I ask the same question more plainly—if, indeed, I can ask it any more plainly: is it, or is it not, your opinion that the wise man knows wisdom?"

"If it is possible," he replied, "to find a wise man such as reason conceives of, I can believe that he knows wisdom."

"Reason, therefore," I said, "indicated to you that the wise man is such that he knows wisdom. So far you are right. You could not have properly held any other opinion."

10. "And now I ask you if the wise man can be found. If he can, then he can also know wisdom and our discussion is finished. But if you say that he cannot be found, then the question will be, not if the wise man knows any-

thing, but rather if any one can be a wise man. Answering this in the affirmative, we must take leave of the Academics, and go over this point with you as far as we can, and with great care and attention. For the Academics maintained, or rather opined, at one and the same time that the wise man could exist, but that, nevertheless, man could not attain to knowledge. Therefore, they actually claimed that the wise man knows nothing. But you believe that he knows wisdom, which certainly is not identical with knowing nothing. For we are agreed, as are all the ancients and even the Academics themselves, that no one can know what is not true. Accordingly, there remains now that you either maintain that wisdom is nothing, or admit that the wise man as described by the Academics is such as is unknown to reason, and then, dropping that question, agree to investigate if man can possess such wisdom as is conceived by reason. For there is no other wisdom which we should, or can, rightly call by that name."

CHAPTER 5

The Question of Assent

11. "Even though I should concede," he said, "what you are so anxiously striving for, namely, that the wise man knows wisdom, and that between us we have discovered something which the wise man can know, nevertheless, I do not at all think that the whole case of the Academics has been undermined. Indeed, I notice that they can fall back on a stronghold that is by no means weak, and that their line of retreat has not been cut off. They can still withhold assent. In fact, the very point in

which you think they have been vanquished, helps their
cause. For they will say that it is so true that nothing can
be known and that assent must be withheld from every-
ting, that even this their principle of not being able to
know anything, which practically from the very beginning
until you came along, they had maintained as probable, is
now wrested from them by your argument.[9] Your argument may be in fact invincible or may seem so to me in my
stupidity, but as before, so now, it cannot dislodge them,
when they can still with confidence assert that even now
assent must be withheld from everything. It is possible,
they will say, that perhaps some day they themselves or
some one else will discover some argument which can be
urged with point and probability against this second principle of theirs also. They would have us notice that their
behaviour is illustrated and mirrored, so to speak, by that
of Proteus who, it is said, could be caught only by means
which invariably did not result in his capture. His pur-
suers were never sure that what they had was still he,
unless some divinity informed them.[10] May that divinity be
present to us, and may he deign to show us that truth for
which we strive so hard! I, too, shall then confess, even
if the Academics do not agree—though I think they will—
that they have been overcome."

12. "Good!" I said, "that was all I wanted. For, look,
I beg you, at all the great gains I have made! First, we
can say that the Academics are so far vanquished that they
have now no defence left except the impossible. Indeed,
who could in any way understand or believe that a man
who is beaten, by the very fact that he has been beaten,
boasts that he has won? And so, if we have any further

dispute with them, it is not on the score of their assertion that nothing can be known, but on the score of their maintaining that one must not assent to anything.

"Consequently, we are now in agreement. For both they and I believe that the wise man knows wisdom. But they advise, all the same, that assent should not be given to this. They say that they *believe* only, but do not at all *know.* As if I should profess that I *know!* I say that I also *believe* this. If they do not know wisdom, then they, and I with them, are stupid. But I think that we should approve of something, namely, truth. I ask them if they deny this, that is to say, if they declare that one must not assent to truth. They will never say this; but they will maintain that truth cannot be found. Consequently, in this I am to a great extent at one with them in so far as both of us do not object, and, therefore, necessarily agree, to the proposition that one must assent to truth.

" 'But who will indicate truth for us?' they ask. On that point I shall not trouble to dispute with them. I am satisfied since they consider it no longer probable that the wise man knows nothing. Otherwise, they would be forced to maintain a most absurd proposition, that either wisdom is nothing, or the wise man does not know wisdom.

CHAPTER 6

Truth Revealed only by a Divinity

13. "You, Alypius, have told us who it is that can point out truth—and I must take pains to disagree with you as little as possible. You remarked that only some divinity [11]

could reveal truth to man. Your words were brief but full of piety. There has been nothing in our discussion which has given me more delight, nothing more profound, nothing more probable, and, provided, so I trust, that divinity be present to us, nothing more true. With what profound understanding and sensitiveness to what is best in philosophy did you direct our attention to Proteus! Proteus, of whom you all know, is introduced as a symbol of truth. You will see, young men, from this that the poets are not entirely despised by philosophy. Proteus, as I say, plays in poetry the role of truth which no one can hold if, deceived by false representations, he slackens or lets loose the bonds of understanding. It is these representations which, because of our association with corporeal things, do their best to fool and deceive us through the senses which we use for the necessities of this life, even when we have already grasped truth and hold it, so to speak, within our hands.

"Here, then, is the third blessing which has come upon me, and I cannot find words to express how highly I value it. I find my most intimate friend agreeing with me not only on probability as a factor in human life, but also on religion itself—a point which is the clearest sign of a true friend; for friendship has been rightly and with just reverence defined as 'agreement on things human and divine combined with goodwill and love.' [12]

CHAPTER 7

Augustine's Refutation of the New Academy

14. "Nevertheless, lest the arguments of the Academics should seem somewhat to cloud the issue, or we ourselves seem to some to dispute arrogantly the authority of highly learned men, among whom Tullius especially must always have weight with us, I shall with your leave first put forward a few considerations against those who would believe that the arguments referred to stand in the way of truth. Then I shall show why, as it seems to me, the Academics concealed their real doctrine. Now, then, Alypius, although I see that you are entirely on my side, nevertheless take a brief for them for a few moments, and answer my question."

"Since," he replied, "you have, as they say, got off on the right foot to-day, I shall not do anything to hinder your complete victory. I shall with the greater confidence attempt to defend their side, seeing that the task is one imposed by yourself. All the same, I would prefer you, if you find it convenient, to achieve the result you aim at rather by means of an uninterrupted discussion than by this questioning, lest, although already your prisoner, I should be tormented, as being in fact an unyielding enemy, by the rack of all your detailed arguments. Such cruelty is not at all in accordance with your humanity!"

15. And so I, when I noticed that the others, too, wanted this, began, as it were, anew. "I shall do as you wish," I said, "although I had hoped that after my toil in

the rhetoric school,[13] I should find some rest in this light armour—that is, I should conduct these enquiries by question and answer rather than by exposition—nevertheless, since we are so few and it will not be necessary for me to raise my voice beyond what is good for my health, and since I have also wished that the pen should, so to speak, guide and control my discourse—also on account of my health, lest I become more excited mentally than is good for my body—listen, then, to my opinion, given to you, as you wish, in continuous exposition.[14]

In the first place, however, let us examine a point about which the enthusiastic supporters of the Academics are very boastful. There is in the books which Cicero wrote in support of them a certain passage that to me seems seasoned with rare wit, while some think it a passage of great power and conviction. It would be hard to imagine that any man should not be impressed by what is there written: [15]

Everybody of every other school that claims to be wise, gives the second place to the wise man of the Academy. It is inevitable, of course, that each claims the first place for himself. From this one can conclude with probability that the Academic rightly judges himself as holding the first place, since in the judgment of all the others he holds the second.

16. Suppose, for example, that there is a Stoic wise man present. It was against the Stoics especially that the Academics felt called upon to pit their wits. If Zeno or Chrysippus [16] be asked who is the wise man, he will reply that it is the man whom he himself has described. But Epicurus [17] or some other adversary will deny this, and maintain that his own representative rather, one who is as skilled as a bird-catcher in catching pleasure, is the wise man. The fight is on! Zeno shouts, and the whole Porch is in uproar: man was born for nothing else but virtue; she draws souls to herself merely by her grandeur, without resorting to the bait of any external ad-

vantage and, as it were, of a pandering reward; the pleasure vaunted by Epicurus is a thing received in common by beasts and by them alone; to pitch out man—and the wise man!—into such company is abominable.

But over against this, Epicurus, like another Bacchus, calling from his Gardens a horde to aid him, who, though drunk, yet look for someone whom in their Bacchic frenzy, they can tear to pieces with their long nails and savage fangs, and exploiting the popular approval of pleasure and an easy-going and quiet life, maintains passionately that without pleasure nobody could appear to be happy.

Should an Academic chance upon their quarrel, he will listen to each side as it attempts to win him over to itself. But if he joins one side or the other, he will be shouted down by the side he is leaving in the lurch, as crazy, ignorant, and reckless. Accordingly, when he has given an attentive ear now to this side, now to that, and is asked his opinion, he will say that he is in doubt. Now ask the Stoic, which is the better—Epicurus who declares that the Stoic is talking nonsense, or the Academic who gives the verdict that he must give further consideration to a matter of such moment—and no one doubts but that the Academic will be preferred. And next turn to Epicurus and ask him which he prefers—Zeno by whom he is called a beast, or Arcesilas who tells him: "Perhaps what you say is true, but I shall have to look into the matter more closely." Is it not clear that Epicurus will decide that the whole Porch is crazy, and that in comparison with them, the Academics are unassuming and judicious people?

"Quite similarly, regarding practically all the other philosophical sects Cicero treats his readers to what we might call a delightful piece of theatre. He shows, as it were, that there is none of those sects which, having of necessity put itself in the first place, does not proclaim that it allots the second place to the one which it sees is not in opposition to, but merely undecided about, its own position. On that point I shall not oppose them in any way or deprive them of any glory.

CHAPTER 8

17. "Some people, to be sure, may think that in this passage Cicero was not poking fun, but rather that because he was appalled by the levity of these Greeklings, he purposed to dig up and collect some of their banalities and rantings. But if I wished to join issue with such pretence, could I not easily show how much less an evil it is to have no knowledge than to be incapable of receiving any? Thus it happens that if this petty boaster of the Academics offers himself as a pupil to the various sects, and none of them succeeds in convincing him of what it thinks it knows, they will then all come together with a will and make a mockery of him. For now each of them will judge that every other adversary has not indeed learnt anything, but that the Academic is *incapable* of learning anything. After that he will be driven from one school after the other not with the rod, which would cause him a little more shame than hurt, but by the clubs and cudgels of the men of the mantle.[18] For there will be no trouble in calling in the help of the Cynics,[19] as one would call in Hercules, to overcome the common scourge.

"And if I, who may be more easily allowed to do so, seeing that though I practise philosophy I am not yet wise, wish to compete with the Academics for the contemptible glory that is theirs, how can they halt me? Suppose that an Academic and myself together came upon the conflict of philosophers described before. Let all be present. Let them expound their opinions briefly in the time allowed. Ask Carneades his opinion. He will reply that he is in doubt. Promptly each will prefer him to all the others; that is to say, all will prefer him among all the others—truly a distinction great and remarkable!

"Who would not like to achieve a like distinction? And so, when I am asked my opinion, I, too, shall give the same answer. I shall be equally commended. That is to say, the glory which the wise man is reaping is of the sort that equates him with the blockhead! But suppose the latter easily beats him in his distinction: will not the Academic be put to shame? As he is trying to slip off from the trial, I shall pull him back—for stupidity surpasses itself in craving for a victory of this kind. Holding him tight, I shall tell the judges something which they do not know, and say: 'Gentlemen, there is this much in common between this fellow and myself, that neither of us knows which of you follows truth. But we have also individual opinions of our own, about which I ask you to enter a judgment. I, for my part, am uncertain, although I have heard your expositions, as to where truth is, for the simple reason that I do not know which of you is the wiser. But this fellow denies that even the wise man knows anything, even wisdom itself, to which he owes it that he is called wise!'

"Can anybody fail to see who will win the palm? If my opponent admits my charge, I shall best him in glory. But if he blushes for shame and confesses that the wise man does know wisdom, then my opinion carries the day.

CHAPTER 9

18. "However, let us now retire from this courthouse with its wranglings and betake ourselves somewhere where no crowd will disturb us. If only it could be the school [20] itself of Plato, which is said to have received its name from the fact that it was cut off from the public! But let us no longer talk about glory, which is a thing of little and trifling account, but rather, so far as we can, of life itself and what hope there is of happiness.

"The Academics deny that anything can be known. How have you established this, you men of learning and scholarship? 'Zeno's definition,' they say, 'taught us that.' But why I beg you? If it is true, then a man who knows merely it itself, knows some truth. If it is not true, then it should not have upset men of such calibre. But let us examine what Zeno says: according to him that object of sense can be comprehended and perceived, which manifests itself by signs that cannot belong to what is not true. Was it this that moved you, my dear Platonist, to use every endeavour to draw those interested away from the hope of learning so that, aided as they were by a shameful lethargy of mind, they might give up the whole business of philosophy?

19. "But why should it not have influenced him profoundly, if nothing such can be found, and unless it be such, cannot be perceived? If this be so, it would have been better to say that man could not possess wisdom than that the wise man should not know why he lives, should not know how he lives, should not know if he lives, and

finally—than which nothing more perverse, silly and crazy could be said—that he should be wise and at the same time be ignorant of wisdom. Which is the more shocking statement to bear, that man cannot be wise, or that the wise man does not know wisdom? There can be no use in discussing the point further, if the matter itself so explained does not offer the necessary basis for a decision. But the chance is that if the former statement were made, men would be driven away entirely from philosophy. In view of this, are they to be attracted to her by the august and alluring name of wisdom that later, having wasted their lives and learnt nothing, they may only heap upon you their greatest curses? For forsaking the pleasures of the body which they might have had, they followed you only into tortures of the mind!

20. "But let us see who it is that most frightens men away from philosophy. Is it he who will say: 'Listen, friend, by philosophy we mean not wisdom itself, but rather the study of wisdom. If you devote yourself to her, you will never indeed be wise while you live here on earth—for wisdom is with God and man cannot possess her—but when you will have sufficiently exercised and purified yourself in this kind of study, your spirit will enjoy wisdom unencumbered after this life, that is, when you will have ceased to be a man'? Or is it he who will say: 'Come, mortal men, to philosophy. Here there is much to be gained. After all, what can be dearer to man than wisdom? Come, then, so that you may become wise—and not know wisdom'? 'I,' he says, 'shall not put it like that.' That is to say, you will deceive; because that exactly represents your position. So it happens that if you do put it like that, they will shun you like a madman; and if you

should win them over in some other way, you would make them mad. But let us take it that men would be equally discouraged from philosophy by either view, if, my friend, Zeno's definition did necessitate some conclusion damaging to philosophy, which should a man be told—something that would grieve him or something that would lead him to make a laughingstock of you?

21. "Nevertheless, let us discuss as best we can — granted that we are not wise—Zeno's definition. 'That sense object,' he says, 'can be comprehended, which so manifests itself that it cannot manifest itself as not true.[21] It is clear that nothing else can be perceived.' 'I, too,' says Arcesilas, 'see this, and it is precisely on this account that I teach that nothing is perceived. For nothing so described can be found.'

"That may be true for you, Arcesilas, and for others who are not wise; but why could it not be found by the wise man? I think, however, that you could give no satisfaction to one—even though he be not wise—who bids you employ your remarkable genius in exploding Zeno's definition, and showing that it, too, can be not true. If you cannot do that, then you have something which you can perceive. But if in fact you do explode it, there is nothing to hinder you from perception. For my part I do not see how it can be exploded and I judge it to be entirely true. Consequently, once I know this much, even though I be not wise, I know something. But suppose it yields to your cleverness: I shall employ the safest disjunction. It must be either true or not true. If it is true, then I am in sound possession of it. If it is not true, then something can be perceived, even though it manifest itself by signs which are shared in common with what is not true. 'But that is impossible,' he says. Well, then, Zeno's definition is entirely true, and anyone who has agreed with him even in this one point only is not guilty of error. Surely, that definition is worthy of the greatest praise and confidence which, while it indicated — in opposition to those who wanted to advance many arguments against the possibility of perception—what kind of thing it was that could be perceived, showed itself at the same time to be that kind of thing. And so it is both a definition and example of things capable of being comprehended. 'Whether or not it be itself true,' says Arcesilas, 'I do not know. But since it is probable, I follow it, and in doing so show that there is nothing such as can, according to it, be comprehended.' You show perhaps that there is nothing such except itself, and you see, I believe, what that means. In any case, even if we were uncertain of it, too, knowledge still does not desert us. For we do know that the definition itself is either true or not true; that is, we know something.

"All the same, Arcesilas will never make me appear ungrateful. It is my considered judgment that that definition is in fact true. For either things which are not true can also be perceived—which the Academics are very much afraid of and which, in fact, is absurd—or, granted that they cannot be perceived, neither can those things be perceived which are very like things which are not true. From which it follows that that definition of Zeno's is true. But now let us turn to what remains to be considered.

CHAPTER 10

The Two Principles of the Academy

22. "Although, unless I am mistaken, what I have said is enough to bring about victory, perhaps I should say more in order to drive my victory home. There are two points put forward by the Academics against which, in so far as we can, we have decided to advance: 'Nothing can be perceived,' and, 'one must not assent to anything.' We shall come later on to the question of assent. For the moment we shall say a few more things about perception.

"Do you people insist that nothing whatever can be comprehended? At this point Carneades woke up—for none of those men slept as lightly as he—and surveyed the evidence of things. As one speaks to oneself, so he, I believe, went on somewhat like this: 'Now, Carneades, are you really going to claim that you do not know whether you are a man or an insect? Will you allow Chrysippus to gloat over you? Let us say that the things that we do not know are those about which *philosophers* inquire. As to *other* things, they do not concern us. If I then stumble in plain, broad daylight, I shall be able to appeal to those obscurities that are impenetrable to the unskilled, and penetrable only to a certain few gifted with eyes that are divine. They, even though they see me in difficulties and falling, cannot betray me to those who are blind, especially when they are also arrogant and too proud to learn.'

"You are getting on nicely, O Greek subtlety, well

equipped and prepared as you are! But you overlook the fact that that principle is at once the formulation of a philosopher, and is placed firmly at the entrance to philosophy. If you attempt to undermine it, the axe with double edge will rebound on to your shins. For if once you shake it, not only can something be perceived, but that, too, can be perceived which is very like that which is not true. Your only chance is to have the courage to do away with it altogether. But it is your lurking-place from which you jump out and pounce fiercely upon the unwary who wish to pass on their way. Some Hercules will strangle you, half-human as you are, in your cave,²² and will crush you with the weight of that principle. For he will show you that there is something in philosophy which cannot be demonstrated by you to be uncertain on the plea that it is like to what is not true.

"I was, it is true, in a hurry to go on to other considerations. Whoever presses me to do so, casts a great slur on you yourself, Carneades, for he supposes that you are as good as dead and can be routed by me on any and every front. But if he does not suppose any such thing, then he is pitiless. For then he leads me on to abandon my fortifications everywhere and to come down to do battle with you on the level plain. Just as I had begun to come down against you, terrified by your mere name, I drew back and cast from my lofty position some kind of a shaft. Whether it reached you, or what it did, let them judge who preside over our conflict. But what a fool am I to have such fear? If I recollect aright, you are dead, and Alypius does not choose to fight as he might, in defence of your grave; and God will readily help me against your ghost.

23. "You say that in philosophy nothing can be perceived, and so that you may give your contention wide
publicity, you seize upon the disputes and disagreements
of philosophers and think with them to furnish arms to
yourself against the philosophers themselves. For how,
you argue, shall we be able to settle the dispute between
Democritus [23] and his predecessors in physics as to
whether there is one or innumerable worlds,[24] when
Democritus himself and his heir, Epicurus, could not
agree? When this latter voluptuary allows the atoms, as
it were his little handmaids, those little bodies which he
joyfully embraces in the dark, to deviate from their course
and turn aside [25] wherever they like into the domains of
others, he is quarrelling and he has thus dissipated all
his patrimony.

"But this is no concern of mine. If it is part of wisdom
to know something of these things, then all this will certainly not escape the attention of the wise man. But if
wisdom consists in something different, then it is *that*
that the wise man knows and the other is despised by him.
Even I, however, who am still far from being anyway
near being a wise man,[26] know something at any rate in
Physics.[27] I am certain, for instance, that there is one
world or not one. If there is not one world, then the
number of worlds is finite or infinite. Carneades may say,
if he likes, that this opinion is like one that is not true.
Likewise, I know that this world of ours is ordered as it
is, either by the intrinsic nature of corporeal matter, or
by some providence; that it either always was and always
will be, or began to be and will never cease, or never
exist forever. I know countless things about physics after
began in time but will end, or began to exist and will not

this manner. These disjunctions are true,[28] and no one can refute them by pointing to any likeness in them to what is not true.

" 'But elect for one member of the disjunction,' bids the Academic. No. I shall not. You are asking me not to assert what I do know, and assert what I do not know. 'But your assertion hangs in the air!' It is better that it should hang there than that it should be dashed to the ground. You see, it is adequate for our purpose; that is to say, as an assertion it can be pronounced either true or not true. I assert that this is something that I know. Let you, who cannot deny that such matter pertains to philosophy, and who assert that none of these things can be known, demonstrate to me that I do not know these things. Assert that these disjunctions are either not true or have something in common with what is not true, so that, as a consequence, they are incapable of being distinguished from what is not true.

CHAPTER 11

Something Can be Perceived

24. " 'But,' he asks, 'how do you know that the world you speak of exists at all? The senses may deceive.' No matter how you argued, you were never able to repudiate the value of the senses to the extent that you could convince us that nothing appears to us to be. Indeed, you have never in any way ventured to try to do so. But you have done your very best to convince us that the reality could be different from the appearance. By the term 'world,' then, I mean all this, whatever kind of thing it

be, which surrounds and nourishes us and which presents itself to my eyes and seems to me to hold earth and sky or quasi-earth and quasi-sky. If you say that non-reality presents itself to me, I shall still be free from error. It is he who rashly judges that which presents itself to him to be actual reality that falls into error. But while you do say that what is not true can present itself to sentient beings, you do not say that non-reality so presents itself. Indeed, all ground for disputation—wherein you love to reign supreme—is entirely removed if not only we know nothing, but if no appearance presents itself to us. If, however, you deny that that which presents itself to me is the world, you are raising a question merely about a word; for I have stated that I do call that appearance the 'world.'

25. "But you will ask me: 'If you are asleep,[29] does the world which you now see exist?' I have already said that whatever presents itself to me in that way, I call 'world.' But if you wish that only to be called 'world' which presents itself to those who are awake or, even better, those who are sane, then maintain also, if you can, that those who are asleep or insane are not insane and asleep in the world! Accordingly, I make this statement: all that mass and contrivance in which we are, whether we be sleeping, or insane, or awake, or sane, is either one or not one. Explain how that judgment can be not true. If I am asleep, possibly I have made no statement at all. Or, if in my sleep the words have, as happens, escaped my mouth, possibly I have not spoken them here, sitting as I am, and with this audience. But the proposition itself that I have mentioned cannot be not true.

"And I am not saying that I have perceived this on condition of my being awake. For you could say that in my sleep, too, this could have presented itself to me, and, consequently, can be very like what is not true. But it is manifest that no matter in what condition I am, if there is one world and six worlds, there are in all seven worlds, and I unhesitatingly assert that I know this. Now, then, convince me that this combination or the above-mentioned disjunctions can be not true by reason of sleep, madness, or the unreliability of the senses; and if being awakened from my slumber I recall them, I shall allow that I am vanquished. I feel sure that it is now sufficiently clear what appearances, although not true, can because of sleep or insanity present themselves as true: they are those which pertain to bodily senses. For that three times three makes nine, and that this is the squaring of rational numbers, must be true even though the human race were snoring! [30] All the same, I notice that much can be said in defence even of the senses themselves—things which we do not find to be questioned by the Academics. The senses are not, I take it, blamed for the fact that insane people have illusions, or that we see in our dreams things that are not true. If the senses give reports that are true to those who are awake and sane, then they will not be involved in what the mind of one who is asleep or insane, conjures up.

26. "There remains to ask if, when the senses report, they report what is true. Now, then, if an Epicurean says: 'I have no complaint to make about the senses. It is unjust to demand from them more than that of which they are capable. When the eyes see anything, they see

what is true': is, then, what the eyes see of an oar in water, true?[31] Certainly, it is true. A cause has intervened so that it should present itself so. If when an oar was dipped under water it presented itself as straight, then in that case I would convict my eyes of giving a report that was not true. For they would not see what, given the existing circumstances, should have been seen. What need is there of developing the theme? The same thing can be said of towers that appear to move, of the changing colours on the feathers of birds, and of countless other cases.

" 'But,' says someone, 'I am deceived, if I give my assent.' Do not assent more than that you know that it appears so to you.[32] There is then no deception. I do not see how the Academic can refute him who says: I know that this presents itself to me as white; I know that this delights my ear; I know that this has a sweet smell for me; I know that this has a pleasant taste for me; I know that this feels cold to me. 'Tell me, rather, if the leaves of the wild olive tree, of which the goat is so passionately fond, are *per se* bitter?' You rascal! The goat himself is more reasonable! I do not know how cattle find them. Anyway, I find them bitter. Does that satisfy you? 'But there is perhaps among men one to whom they are not bitter.' You are trying to make a nuisance of yourself. Have I said that all men found them bitter? I said that I found them bitter now, and I do not even assert that they will always be so for me. Could it not happen that at different times and for different reasons a thing could taste in one's mouth now sweet, now bitter? This I do assert that when a man tastes something, he can swear in all good faith that he knows that to his palate a given thing is sweet or the contrary. No Greek sophistry can steal such knowledge from him. Who would be so impertinent as to say to me as I savour with delight the taste of something: 'Perhaps there is nothing to taste; you are only dreaming'? Do I stop my savouring? No! I reply that even though I were dreaming, it would still delight me. Accordingly, no likeness to what is not true can prove that that which I said I knew was wrong. Moreover, an Epicurean or the Cyrenaics [33] may perhaps say many other things in defence of the senses, and I am not aware that the Academics have said anything to refute them. But what is that to me? If they want to, and if they can, let them refute these things. I shall even help them.

"Certainly, their arguments against sense perception are not valid against all philosophers. There are some philosophers, for example, who maintain that whatever the spirit receives by way of bodily sense can generate opinion indeed, but not knowledge.[34] They insist that the latter is found only in the intelligence [35] and, far removed from the senses, abides in the mind. Perhaps the wise man whom we seek is to be found in their midst. But we shall talk about this at another time. Now let us turn to the points that remain. In view of what has already been said, we shall, if I mistake not, be able to deal with them in a few words.

CHAPTER 12

27. "What help or hindrance can bodily sense be in the consideration of Ethics? Those who put man's true and greatest good in pleasure, are not prevented by the dove's neck, or the cry that is doubtful, or the weight that is heavy for a man but light for a camel, or a thousand other such things, from saying that they know that they find pleasure in that in which they find pleasure, and are displeased by that by which they are displeased—and I do not see how this can be refuted. Can it be that these things influence him who places the ultimate good in the mind?

" 'Which of these two opinions do you yourself choose?' If you ask me my opinion, I think that in the mind is to be found man's supreme good.[36] Now, however, we are talking about knowledge. Go, then, and question the wise man, who must know wisdom. But in the meantime I, who am such a dullard and ignoramus, am able to know the ultimate good of man, wherein is happiness: either there is none, or it is in the spirit, or in the body, or in both. Prove, if you can, that I do not know this. Your celebrated arguments can do nothing. And if you cannot do this—for you will not be able to find anything not true to which it bears likeness—shall I hesitate to conclude that my opinion that the wise man knows whatever in philosophy is true is correct, since I myself already know in philosophy many things that are true?

28. " 'But perhaps the wise man is afraid lest he should choose the ultimate good while he is asleep.' No danger

at all! When he awakes, he will, if it displeases him, repudiate, and if it pleases, retain it.[37] Who can justly
blame him for having seen in a dream something that was
not true? Or perhaps you will be afraid lest while he is
asleep, if he assents to what is not true as true, he lose
his wisdom? Indeed, not even one who is asleep would
dare to dream that he should call a man wise if he were
awake, but deny that he is such if he were to sleep.

"The same things hold for the question of insanity.
Though I am anxious to hurry on to other things, I shall,
however, before I go, leave an irrefutable statement on
the point: either a man's wisdom is lost because of his
madness, in which case he will no longer be the wise man,
who, you insist, does not know truth; or his knowledge
remains in his intellect, even though the rest of his mind
represents as if in a dream what it has received from
the senses.

CHAPTER 13

29. "There remain Dialectics. The wise man certainly
knows this well, and no one can know what is not true.
But if he does not know dialectics, then the knowledge
of dialectics does not pertain to wisdom, seeing that he
can be wise without it. Moreover, it is superfluous for
us to ask whether it be true or can be perceived.

"Some one may say to me at this point: 'Well, stupid,
you usually tell us whatever you know. Were you not able
to know anything about dialectics?' I know more about
it than about any other part of philosophy. In the first
place, it was dialectics that taught me that all the propo-

sitions which I have indicated already were true. Again, through dialectics I have come to know many other true things. 'Enumerate them for us, if you can.' If there are four elements in the world, there are not five. If there is one sun, there are not two. The same soul cannot both die and be immortal. A man cannot at the same time be happy and not happy. Here and now there is not day and night at the same time. We are now either awake or asleep. What I seem to see is either body or not body. These and many other things which would take too long to mention, I have learned through dialectics to be true. They are true in themselves no matter what state our senses are in. Dialectics taught me that if, of any one of the conditional statements which I have just mentioned, the first part be assumed as true, it necessarily involves the truth of the dependent part.[38] But the propositions involving contrariety or disjunction which I enunciated, are of this nature that when a part is taken away, whether that be composed of one or more things, something is left which by the removal is made certain. Dialectics also taught me that when there is agreement about the matter on account of which words are employed, then one should not dispute about the words. If one does that through inexperience, then one should be taught. If one does it through malice, then one should be ignored. If one is incapable of being taught, one should be advised to do something else than waste one's time and labour in trifling. If one does not take the advice, then one should be abandoned to one's fate.

"Concerning specious and fallacious reasonings there is a short principle of behaviour: if they come about as a result of an unwise concession, then one should return to what one has conceded. If truth and falsehood are found in conflict in one and the same statement, one should conclude on what one understands, and not bother about what cannot be explained. But if the 'how' of certain things escapes man entirely, then one should not seek the knowledge of it.

"All these things and many others, which it is unnecessary to recall, dialectics have taught me, and certainly I must not be ungrateful. The wise man either ignores all these or, if a thorough knowledge of dialectics is the knowledge itself of truth, he will know it so well that in contempt, and without any weakening, he will destroy, if only by ignoring it, that most fallacious sophism of the Academics: 'If it is true, it is not true; if it is not true, it is true.'

"I think this will be enough on the question of perception, especially since the whole case will be dealt with again when I come to speak of the matter of assent.

CHAPTER 14

Assent Can be Given

30. "And now, therefore, let us come to a point on which Alypius still seems to be in doubt. First, let us see what it is that makes you so careful and exacting. 'If the opinion of the Academics that the wise man knew nothing, confirmed as it was'—these are your own words—'by so many powerful arguments, is overthrown by your discovery, whereby we are compelled to admit that it is

much more probable that the wise man knows wisdom, then all the more should we refuse to assent. For by this itself is it demonstrated that nothing can be advocated—even though the arguments used be ever so copious and neatly pointed—which cannot also, granted sufficient ingenuity, be controverted with equal if not greater acuteness. And so it happens that the moment he is beaten, the Academic has won.'

"Would that he were beaten! No matter what Pelasgic [40] trick he uses, he will never succeed in leaving the field victorious when he has been beaten by me. Of course, if nothing else can be found to counter this argument, of my own free motion I, too, allow that I am beaten. For we are not interested in covering ourselves with glory but in the finding of truth. I am content if by any means I can cross over that barrier which confronts those who are beginning philosophy. [41] It piles up darkness from some hidden source, and warns that the whole of philosophy is obscure, and does not allow one to hope that any light will be found in it.

"For my part, I desire nothing more if it is now probable that the wise man knows something. It seemed probable that he should withhold his assent for no other reason than that it was probable that nothing could be perceived: when that reason has disappeared—the wise man perceives, as is conceded, at least wisdom herself—no reason any longer will remain, why the wise man should not assent at least to wisdom. Obviously, it is without any doubt even more monstrous that the wise man should not assent to wisdom than that he should not know her.

31. "But let us now, if you will and if that be possible,

picture to ourselves the spectacle of a fight, so to speak, between the wise man and wisdom. Wisdom says (and what else should she say?) that she is wisdom. He replies, 'I do not believe it.' Who is it that says to wisdom, 'I do not believe that you are wisdom'? Who, but he with whom she could talk and in whom she deigned to dwell— that it to say, the wise man?

"Now go and fetch me to engage in a conflict with the Academics. There! a new fight is on! The wise man and wisdom are fighting! The wise man does not want to give in to wisdom! I shall stand aside with you and await the issue without anxiety; for who does not believe that wisdom is invincible? All the same, let us strengthen our position with some argument. In this conflict either the wise man of the Academics conquers wisdom, in which case he will be conquered by me—for he will not be the wise man; or he will be conquered by her, in which case we shall teach that the wise man assents to wisdom. That is to say, either the Academic wise man is not a wise man at all, or the wise man will assent to something—unless, of course, he who was ashamed to say that the wise man did not know wisdom, will not be ashamed to say that the wise man does not assent to wisdom! But if it is now probable that the wise man perceives at least wisdom herself, and there is no longer any reason why he should not assent to that which he can perceive, I conclude that what I wanted is probable, namely, that the wise man will assent to wisdom.

"If you ask me, where he will find wisdom herself, I shall reply: in his own very self. If you say that he does not know what is in himself, you are returning once again to the ridiculous proposition that the wise man does not know wisdom. If you say that the wise man himself cannot be found, then our dispute will be, not with the Academics, but with you whoever you are that hold this, and on another occasion. When these men engage in this type of discussion, they deal with it as certainly referring to the case of the wise man. Cicero exclaims that as for himself, he is a man of many opinions only, but that he is discussing the case of the wise man. If you were unaware of this, young men, you must have read in the *Hortensius:* 'If, then, nothing is certain and the wise man must not have opinion merely, the wise man will never give assent.' [42] From this it is clear that in those disputations of theirs against which we are contending, they are dealing with the case of the wise man.

32. "I, therefore, think that the wise man has sure possession of wisdom, that is to say, that the wise man has perceived wisdom, and, consequently, that he does not have opinions merely, when he assents to wisdom. For he assents to that which if he did not perceive, he would not be a wise man. The Academics, in fact, do not prohibit anyone from assenting except to things which cannot be perceived. Wisdom is not nothing. When, then, the wise man knows wisdom, and assents to wisdom, he does not know nothing, and does not assent to nothing.

"Do you wish for more? Shall we discuss briefly that error which the Academics say can be entirely avoided if assent does not draw the mind to anything at all? They say that not only he errs who assents to what is not true, but also he who assents to what is doubtful, even though it be in fact true. For my part, I find nothing that is not doubtful. But the wise man finds, as we were saying, wisdom herself.

CHAPTER 15

The "Probable" Insufficient and Dangerous

33. "But perhaps, you are now asking me to leave my own ground. One should be careful about leaving a position that is safe. We are dealing with men who are crafty indeed. Nevertheless, I shall do as you bid me. But what shall I say at this point? Indeed, what am I to say? Tell me, what can I say? I shall have to use the old stock argument for which they have a stock reply. What else can I do, seeing that you have compelled me to leave my stronghold? Shall I appeal to the help of the learned, so that if I am vanquished in their company, I shall perhaps be less ashamed of being beaten? I shall with all my strength, then, hurl at them a weapon which though now rusty and musty with age, is, unless I am mistaken, all the same a very effective one: 'He who does not assent to anything, does nothing.' [43] 'You ignoramus! What about the "probable"? What about "what-is-like-truth"?' There you are! That is what you were looking for! Do you hear the clash of Grecian shields? The shock of my weapon, great as it was, has been withstood; and with what force did we hurl it! And my supporters can offer me nothing more potent and, as far as I can see, we have inflicted no trace of a wound. I shall turn for help to the homely weapons offered me by the farm. The heavier ones only weigh me down and are of no help to me.

34. "When at my leisure here in the country I had been thinking for a long time how it was that what they

call 'probable' or 'what-is-like-truth' could prevent our acts from error, at first it seemed to me—as it had seemed when I taught such things for money [44]—that the matter was nicely established and defended against attack. But then as I examined the whole position more carefully, I thought I saw one way by which error could come in upon those who felt so secure. For I think that not only does he err who follows the wrong track, but he also who does not follow the right one.

"To illustrate, let us picture two men travelling to one place. One of them has resolved not to believe anyone; the other believes everyone. They come to a place where the road forks. The credulous traveller addresses a shepherd or some rustic standing on the spot: 'Hello, my good man. Tell me, please, which is the best way to that place?' The reply: 'If you take this road, you will not go wrong.' He says to his companion: 'What he says is correct. Let us go this way.' The careful traveller laughs and makes a fool of the other for having given assent so quickly. While the other takes his way, he remains at the junction of the roads. He is beginning to feel foolish himself because of his hesitation, when from the road not taken by his companion there appears and draws near an elegant and refined gentleman riding on horseback. The traveller rejoices. He salutes the man as he approaches, and tells him what is on his mind. He asks him the way. Not only that—he tells him why he has delayed so that by indicating his preference for him rather than for the shepherd, he may make him the better disposed to himself. He, however, happens to be an arrant knave, one of those fellows now commonly called *samardoci*.[45] The scoundrel indulges in his usual practice, and that, too, without charging a penny: 'Go this way,' he says. 'I have just come from there.' So, he deceives him and passes on his way.

"But our traveller would not be deceived! 'Indeed,' he says, 'I shall not assent to his information as true. But since it is probable, and since to do nothing here is neither proper nor useful, I shall go the way he indicates.' Meanwhile he who erred in assenting, too quickly judging that the shepherd's words were true, is already resting in the place for which they set out. But he who has not erred, since he follows the 'probable,' is lost in some woods and has not yet found anybody who knows the place where he proposed to go!

"Really, I must tell you that when I was thinking over these things, I could not keep from laughing. To think that the doctrine of the Academics somehow brings it about that he should err, who is on the right road—even though it be by chance—but that he, who following probability is led over impassable mountains and does not get where he wants to go, should not seem to err! To show, quite justly, my disapproval of rash assent, I should say that both erred, rather than that the second traveller did not err. And so being more on my guard against the Academic doctrine, I began to consider the deeds of men and their principles of behaviour. Then, indeed, I discovered so many and such fundamental grounds against the Academics that I could no longer laugh, but was half angry and half sorrowful that men so learned and intelligent should have descended to such criminal and shameful doctrine.

CHAPTER 16

35. "It may be, indeed, that not everyone who errs, commits sin. It is conceded, however, that everyone who sins, either errs or does something worse. Well, then, if some young man, hearing the Academics say: 'It is shameful to err, and, consequently, we ought not to assent to anything; when, however, a man does what seems probable to him, he neither sins, nor errs. All he need remember is that he is not to assent to as true anything that comes before his mind or senses'—if, I say, he hears this, what if the young man will lay siege to the chastity of another's wife?

"I am asking you, Marcus Tullius—yes, you—for your opinion. We are dealing with the morals and lives of young men, with whose formation and instruction all your writings are concerned. What can you say but that it is not probable to *you*, that the young man would do such a thing? But to *him*, it is probable. For if we were to live by what seemed probable to another, you ought not to have governed in the state, since Epicurus thought that one should not do such a thing. That young man will, then, commit adultery with another's wife. If he is caught, where will he find you to defend him? And even if he does find you, what will you say? You will deny outright that the thing happened. But if it is so clear that it is useless to deny it? Of course, you will try to convince your opponents, as if you were in a scholastic establishment at Cumae or Naples, that he had committed no sin, in fact, had not even erred. He did not assent to the proposition that 'I should commit adultery' as true. But then it occurred to him as probable: he followed it—he did the deed. Or, perhaps he did not do it, but thinks he has done it! The husband in his simplicity is causing general confusion by his litigation and the clamour he raises about his wife's chastity—with whom he is perhaps now sleeping without being aware of it!

"If the jury is able to follow this, they will either ignore the Academics and mete out punishment on the crime as having been actually committed, or, being convinced by the same gentlemen, they will, acting according to what is likely and probable, condemn the man, so that his advocate will now be at a complete loss as to what course to take. He will not have cause to get angry with any of them, since all say that they have not fallen into an error. For, while not assenting, they had done what seemed probable. In these circumstances he will lay aside the role of advocate and assume that of the consoling philospher. He can thus readily persuade the young man, who has already made such progress in the Academy, to think that he is condemned only in a dream.

"But you think I am making fun! I am prepared to swear by all that is holy [46] that I am completely at a loss to know how that young man sinned, if one who does what seems probable to him, does not sin. The only possible answer I find is that they may say that to err and to sin are two entirely different things and that by their principles they had in mind that we should not err, while they considered sinning itself to be of no great consequence.

36. "I pass over homicide, parricide, sacrilege, and

every type of crime and evildoing that can be committed
or thought of—all can be justified by a few words, and,
what is worse, before judges that are wise: 'I did not
assent, and therefore I did not err. How could I not have
done what seemed probable?' If anyone thinks that such
arguments cannot be made to seem probably conclusive,
let him read the speech of Catiline [47] wherein he sought
to commend the parricide of one's country, in which is
embodied all crime.

"But what follows is merely ridiculous. The Academics
themselves say that they act only on the probable. Nevertheless, they make great efforts in searching for truth,
although they have already made up their minds that it
is probable that it cannot be found. What a marvellous
absurdity! But let us forget about it: it does not affect us
or endanger our lives or belongings. But the other point
is of the greatest importance: it is fraught with the most
serious consequences and must cause the greatest anxiety
to every upright man. For if this reasoning of the Academics is probable, then one may commit every crime not
only without being blamed for the sin, but also without
being blamed for an error—since one thought that one
should act on the probable without assenting to anything
as true. Well, then, did the Academics not see this? Indeed, they did see it—for they were clever and careful. I
would never think of claiming that I came anyway near
Marcus Tullius in hard work, prudence, capacity, or learning. Yet, when he says that a man cannot know anything,
if this only were replied: 'I know that it seems to me that
he can,' he would not be able to refute it.

CHAPTER 17

Augustine's Theory of a Secret Doctrine
in the Academy

37. "Why, then, did such great men engage in per-
petual and stubborn wranglings in order that no one
might seem to possess the knowledge of truth? Listen
now a little more carefully, not to what I know, but to
what I think.[48] I kept this to the last so that I might be
able to explain if I could, the whole policy [49] of the Academics as it appears to me.

"Plato, the wisest and most learned man of his day, who
spoke in such fashion that whatever he said became important, and said such things that no matter how he
should say them they could not be of little importance, is
said to have learned after the death of his master Socrates,
whom he deeply loved, many things from the Pythago-
reans [50] also. Pythagoras,[51] for his own part, had not been
satisfied with Greek philosophy, which then hardly
existed, or, at any rate, was very obscure, and having been
moved by the disputations of a certain Pherecydes, of
Syros,[52] so as to believe that the spirit was immortal,
travelled abroad far and wide listening to the wisdom of
many wise men. Plato added to Socrates' ethics with its
wit and subtlety, the knowledge of things natural and
divine, which he with great care had acquired from those
whom I have mentioned, and imposing upon both, as a
co-ordinator and judge, dialectics, which is either itself
wisdom or that without which wisdom is absolutely im-

possible, is said to have put together a complete system of philosophy, which we have not time to discuss now. It is enough for my purpose that Plato thought that there were two worlds, one intelligible, where truth itself resided, and this sensible world which, it is clear, we apprehend by sight and touch. The first was the true world, while the latter was made like the true world and after its image. Truth, bright and serene, shines from the former in the soul which knows herself; but only opinion, and not knowledge, can be generated from the latter in the souls of those who are not wise. Whatever was done in this world according to the virtues that Plato termed 'civil'—virtues that are like the other real virtues which are known by a few wise men only—could not be called anything but 'like-the-truth.'

38. "These and other similar things, I believe, were preserved, as far as possible, by his successors and guarded as 'mysteries.' [53] For neither are such things easily understood save only by those who, purifying themselves from every vice, live a life at a level higher than is human; nor would he be without grave fault who, knowing them, would wish to teach them to men of any kind whatever. I suspect that Zeno, the first of the Stoics, when he came to the school left behind by Plato and then presided over by Polemo,[54] was regarded with suspicion, because he had already received and believed certain other doctrines, and did not seem to be one to whom the Platonic teachings, hallowed as they were, could be presented and entrusted, until he had forsaken those doctrines which he had brought with him from elsewhere to the Platonic school.

"Polemo dies and Arcesilas succeeds him. Arcesilas,

while being a fellow student with Zeno, had been instructed by Polemo. Accordingly, when Zeno, fascinated by a certain opinion of his own concerning the world, and especially the soul (whose interests true philosophy is always vigilant to defend), began to say that the soul was mortal, and that there is nothing beyond the present world of the senses and nothing transpires in it except through corporeal agency—he believed, for instance, that God Himself was just fire—Arcesilas, in my opinion, acted in a most prudent and useful way, since the evil was spreading widely, in concealing completely the doctrine of the Academy and in burying it as gold to be found at some time by posterity. And so, since the multitude is all too liable to rush into false opinions, and people will most readily, however harmfully, believe because of their familiarity with material things, that everything is corporeal, Arcesilas very cleverly, and because he had the interests of men at heart, began to disabuse those of their error whom he found to have been wrongly taught, rather than to teach men who, he decided, could not be taught at all. From these circumstances arose all those teachings which are attributed to the New Academy, teachings for which their predecessors had no need.

39. "Now, if Zeno had but roused himself at length and had seen that nothing could be comprehended except that which answered his definition of what was comprehensible, and that nothing such could be found in things corporeal, to which he attributed everything, this kind of conflict, which, as it happened, unavoidably flared up, would long ago have been extinguished. But Zeno, deceived, as the Academics themselves believed—and I can-

not disagree with them—by the appearance of permanence in things, held on to his contention, and his pernicious doctrine of materialism persisted as well as it could until the time of Chrysippus. This man began to strenghten—for he was well equipped to do so—this doctrine so that it could spread even wider. But on the side of the opponents Carneades fought so much more keenly and prudently than any of his predecessors, that I am amazed that that teaching should afterwards have had any influence at all. For Carneades first abandoned the quibbling sophistry, which, he saw, had reflected very badly upon Arcesilas. In this way he would not seem to want to contradict everything, as it were, for the sake of showing off. Then he set himself the task of destroying utterly the Stoics themselves and Chrysippus.

CHAPTER 18

40. "He was then hard pressed on all sides by the objection that if the wise man assented to nothing he would do nothing. But he—what a man to admire! and yet not so admirable, as he was but drawing on the fountains of Plato—examined the types of actions which his opponents judged commendable, and seeing that they were like certain actions of the true world, he called that which he followed in this world as a rule of action, 'what-is-like-truth.' That to which it was like, he knew well and prudently concealed. He also decided to call 'what-is-like-truth' the 'probable.' A man, indeed, can rightly 'approve' of a representation when he looks upon its exemplar. On

the other hand, how can the wise man approve of, or act on, 'what-is-like-truth,' if he does not know what truth itself is? The Academics therefore, knew what they were doing in approving of things that were in fact not true, but in which they noticed a commendable likeness to truth.[55] But since it was not right or convenient to make known all this, as it were, to the profane, they handed down to their successors, and to such of their contemporaries as they could, some indication of their true doctrine. Whenever an experienced dialectician investigated the terms employed by them, they put him off by reviling and deriding him. For these reasons, then, Carneades is said to have been the founder and chief of a third Academy.

41. "The conflict lasted down to the time of our own Tullius, and, although it had evidently weakened, succeeded with its last gasp in filling Latin letters with an air of unreality. For to my mind nothing could be more unreal than that he should have spoken so copiously and with such great elegance for a point of view which he did not hold. Nevertheless, these windy arguments proved the complete undoing, in my opinion, of that Platonic straw man, Antiochus.[56] (As for the Epicurean herds, these placed their sunny sties in the souls of the voluptuous.) [57] Antiochus was, of course, a pupil of Philo.[58] The latter was, I believe, a prudent man who, because he thought that the enemy was giving up the fight, had begun to open, as it were, the gates, and to recall the Academy to the authority and precepts of Plato. Metrodorus [59] had already tried to do this. He is said to have been the first to admit that the Academics did not sincerely teach that nothing

could be comprehended, but had found it necessary to employ such a weapon against the Stoics.

"Antiochus, then, as I had begun to say, having been a pupil of Philo the Academic and Mnesarchus [60] the Stoic, had, in the guise of a helper and citizen, slipped into the Old Academy, which was as it were bereft of defenders and feeling safe in the belief that there was now no enemy, and brought with him from the cinders of Stoicism a brand of evil to desecrate the shrine of Plato. But Philo, while he lived, had recourse once again to the former weapons in resisting him, and after his death our Tullius completely obliterated whatever remained of the work of Antiochus. For he could not endure, while he had life, that anything that he had loved should be weakened or suffer any infection. Not long after this,[61] then, all obstinacy and pertinacity had died down, and Plato's doctrine, which in philosophy is the purest and most clear, the clouds of error having been removed, shone forth especially in Plotinus. This Platonic philospoher is regarded as being so like Plato, that one would think that they had lived at the same time. The interval of time between them is, however, so great that one should rather think that Plato had come to life again in Plotinus.

CHAPTER 19

Platonism and Christianity

42. "Today, therefore, we see practically no philosophers unless they be either Cynics or Peripatetics [62] or Platonists. The only reason we have the Cynics is that such people find their pleasure in a certain 'freedom' and

even licence in life. But as to that which concerns erudition, doctrine, and morals, all of which help the soul—since there have been acute and clever men who taught in their disputations that Aristotle and Plato in such wise agree with one another [63] that those who are unskilled or examine the matter cursorily think that they disagree—after many generations and many conflicts there is strained out at last, I should say, one system of really true philosophy. For that philosophy is not of this world—such a philosophy our sacred mysteries most justly detest —but of the other, intelligible, world. To which intelligible world the most subtle reasoning would never recall souls blinded by the manifold darkness of error and stained deeply by the slime of the body, had not the most high God, because of a certain compassion for the masses, bent and submitted the authority of the divine intellect even to the human body itself. By the precepts as well as deeds of that intellect souls have been awakened, and are able, without the strife of disputation, to return to themselves and see once again their fatherland.

CHAPTER 20

43. "This theory about the Academics I have sometimes, as far as I could, thought probable. If it is false, I do not mind. It is enough for me that I no longer think that truth cannot be found by man. But if anyone thinks that the Academics were really of this opinion, let him hear Cicero himself. He assures us that the Academics had a practice of hiding their view, and of not revealing it to anyone except to those who lived with them up to old

age.[64] What that doctrine was, God knows! [65] For my part, I do believe that it was Plato's.

"But here in brief is my course of procedure. Whatever be the position of human wisdom, I know that I as yet have not attained it. Though I am in my thirty-third year, I do not think that I should give up hope of reaching it some day. I have renounced everything else that men regard as good, and have proposed to dedicate myself to the search for wisdom. The arguments of the Academics seriously held me back from this quest; but now I feel that in this disputation I have protected myself sufficiently against them. No one doubts but that we are helped in learning by a twofold force, that of authority and that of reason.[66] I, therefore, am resolved in nothing whatever to depart from the authority of Christ—for I do not find a stronger. But as to that which is sought out by subtle reasoning—for I am so disposed as to be impatient in my desire to apprehend truth not only by faith but also by understanding—I feel sure at the moment that I shall find it with the Platonists,[67] nor will it be at variance with our sacred mysteries."

44. At this point they saw that I had finished my discourse. Though night had already come on and some of the record had been written by the light of a lamp, nevertheless the young men were eagerly waiting to see if Alypius would promise to reply—at least on another day. But Alypius said: "I am prepared to assert that nothing has ever pleased me as much as my defeat in to-day's disputation. I think, moreover, that this joy is not something to which I alone am entitled. I communicate it, then, to you, my fellow combatants, or—if you prefer—judges of our contest. Perhaps even the Academics them-

selves wished that in this way they would themselves be vanquished by their descendants! Could we have seen or witnessed anything more charming than the wit of this discourse, more impressive than the weight of its doctrine, more generous than its goodwill, or more skilled than its argumentation? I cannot sufficiently admire the pleasant way in which distasteful subjects were treated; the courage with which hopeless difficulties were faced; the modesty with which conclusions were drawn; and the clarity with which obscure topics were handled. And so, my friends, direct now the expectations with which you were going to have me reply to the argument, to something more worthwhile: join with me in learning. We have a leader who can bring us with God's guidance even to the hidden places of truth."

45. The young men behaved in the manner of children in showing on their faces their disappointment when it was clear that Alypius was not going to reply.

"You are envying the praise given me?" I asked, smiling. "Now that I feel safe about Alypius' constancy and fear him in no way, and so that I may earn your gratitude also, I shall arm you against him who disappointed your eager expectations. Read the *Academica*.[68] You will find there that Cicero—for what could be easier?—has disposed of my trifling arguments.[69] Then do you compel Alypius to defend my discourse against Cicero's invincible arguments! This is the hard return I make you, Alypius, for the praise—undeserved—that you heaped upon me."

They laughed, and so we came to the end—whether or not it was really secure, I do not know—of our long debate on a quieter note and more quickly than I had expected.

NOTES

LIST OF ABBREVIATIONS

ACW	Ancient Christian Writers (Westminster, Maryland 1946-)
CH	A. D. Nock—A. J. Festugière, Corpus Hermeticum (Paris 1945)
CIL	Corpus inscriptionum latinarum
CSEL	Corpus scriptorum ecclesiasticorum latinorum
DTC	Dictionnaire de théologie catholique (Paris 1903-1950)
MGH	Monumenta Germaniae historica
NPNF	Nicene and Post-Nicene Fathers (New York 1890-1912)
OCD	Oxford Classical Dictionary (Oxford 1949)
PL	J. P. Migne, Patrologia latina
RAC	Reallexikon für Antike und Christentum (Leipzig 1941-)
RE	Realenzyklopädie der classischen Altertumswissenschaft (Stuttgart 1894-)
REG	Revue des études grecques
SCA	The Catholic University of America Studies in Christian Antiquity (Washington 1941-)
TWNT	Theologisches Wörterbuch zum Neuen Testament (Stuttgart 1933-)

INTRODUCTION

[1] See Intro. 5 A and nn. 124-27.

[2] This is the spelling found in the manuscripts. The more usual is 'Monica.' There is now, however, a tendency to use the manuscript spelling.

[3] *Conf.* 1. 19; cf. *ibid.* 1. 14. The translation used throughout is Pusey's.

[4] *Ibid.* 1.26 f.

[5] *Ibid.* 2. 5 f.

[6] *Ibid.* 2. 8.

[7] *Ibid.* 3. 6; cf. *ibid.* 3. 7.

[8] *Ibid.* 3. 7, 8. Cf. *ibid.* 6. 18; 8. 17; *De b. vita* 4; *Solil.* 1. 17. For

the influence of this famous book of antiquity on Augustine, cf. J. Stroux, *Augustinus und Ciceros Hortensius* (Berlin-Leipzig 1931) 106-118; A. Claesen, 'Augustinus en Cicero's Hortensius,' *Miscellanea Augustiniana* (Rotterdam 1930) 391-417.

⁹ *Conf.* 3. 9 f.; *De util. cred.* 2.

¹⁰ The question of Augustine's Manichean period is well discussed by P. Alfaric, *L'évolution intellectuelle de saint Augustin* 1 (Paris 1918). It is a question which is not sufficiently stressed in the ordinary biographies of the saint.

¹¹ See Intro. 2 F.

¹² *Conf.* 3. 19; *C. Acad.* 2. 3.

¹³ *Conf.* 4. 1 f.

¹⁴ *Ibid.* 4. 3-6; 7. 8-10.

¹⁵ *Ibid.* 4. 20-23, 27.

¹⁶ *Ibid.* 5. 3, 10-13. For the New Academy, see Intro. 3.

¹⁷ *Ibid.* 5. 14, 22.

¹⁸ *Ibid.* 5. 22.

¹⁹ *Ibid.* 5. 23; cf. *C. Petil.* 3. 30; Possidius, *Vita S. August.* 1. For Symmachus, see O. Seeck, *Q. A. Symmachi quae supersunt*, MGH *Auct. ant.* 6 (Berlin 1883); A. Souter, 'Symmachus' no. 2, OCD 871.

²⁰ Seeck, *op. cit.* cxli; Souter, 'Ausonius,' OCD 126.

²¹ Cf. Seeck, *op. cit. s. vv.*; S. Dill, *Roman Society in the Last Century of the Western Empire* (2nd ed. London 1889) ch. 2.

²² Cf. Claudian, *Panegyricus dictus Manlio Theodoro Consuli* 1-340; A. Ruben, *Dissertatio de vita Fl. Mallii Theodori* (Utrecht 1694); Seeck, *op. cit.* cxliii; Schanz-Hosius-Krüger, *Geschichte der römischen Litteratur* 4 (2nd ed. Munich 1920) 171 f.

²³ Cf. P. Courcelle, *Les lettres grecques en Occident de Macrobe à Cassiodore* (Paris 1948) 122-28, 397 f. The personal influence of people such as Theodorus and other Christians, who were, or had been, sympathetic to Neo-Platonism, upon Augustine at this period needs to be emphasized. The influence of Theodorus, however, can hardly have been as far-reaching as is claimed by Courcelle.

²⁴ 1. 31.

²⁵ 350 is the date usually given.

²⁶ Cf. Claudian, *Paneg. M. Theod.* 24 f. We can gather that these dialogues dealt with the origin and nature of the world, the stars, and the parts of the soul. Augustine in his speculations about the soul in *De b. vita* 5 invites the help of Theodorus in this matter.

²⁷ Cf. W. Liebenam, *Fasti consulares Imperii Romani von 30 v. Chr. bis 565 n. Chr.* (Bonn 1910) 40; Socrates, *Hist. Eccl.* 6. 5, 7.

²⁸ *C. Petil.* 3. 25, 30. In *Conf.* 6. 9 there is mention of another panegyric given by Augustine. Seeck, *op. cit.* cxl, identifies this as that on Bauto; but J. Gibb and W. Montgomery, *The Confessions of Augustine* (Cambridge 1908) 147 note, give reasons for maintaining that there were two panegyrics. On Bauto, see also Seeck, 'Bauto,' RE 3 (1899) 176.

²⁹ Cf. *Conf.* 6. 18.

³⁰ *Ibid.* 6. 9.

³¹ *Ibid.* 6. 3 f., 18.

³² *Ibid.* 6. 19. 'Presidentship' *(praesidatus)*, that is, a governorship.

³³ *Ibid.* 4. 29.

³⁴ *Ibid.* 6. 4 f.

³⁵ Cf. *Solil.* 2. 23.

³⁶ See Intro. 4 A.

³⁷ Gaius Marius Victorinus, who translated the Platonist books read before his baptism by Augustine. We have no evidence that he translated anything of Plotinus. We do know that he translated at least one work of Porphyry's: his *Isagoge*. We possess some of his Christian writings and his explanations of the *De inventione* of Cicero. Cf. O. Bardenhewer, *Geschichte der altkirchlichen Literatur* 3 (2nd ed. Freiburg i. Br. 1923) 460-68.

³⁸ Cf. *C. Acad.* 1. 3; *Conf.* 6.

³⁹ Augustine, *Epist.* 26 *(Ad Licentium)*; 27 *(Ad Paulinum)*; 32 *(Paulinus ad Romanianum et Licentium)*. Cf. n. 30 to Book Two.

⁴⁰ Cf. *C. Acad.* 1. 4, 8, 25; 2. 17, 19 f., 22, 25-29; 3. 6, 45; *De b. vita* 6, 8, 29; *De ord.* 1. 6-8, 20; 2. 28.

⁴¹ *Pagan and Christian Rome* (London 1892) 14 f.

⁴² See below, nn. 151, 155, and 157.

⁴³ 9. 27.

⁴⁴ *Serm.* 356. 3.

⁴⁵ Cf. Alfaric, *op. cit.* 8. n. 1.

⁴⁶ *C. Acad.* 2. 3.

⁴⁷ Augustine, *Epist.* 32. 5. In his own letter to Paulinus, *Epist.* 27. 46, Augustine calls Romanianus a kinsman of Alypius.

⁴⁸ Cf. the Benedictine *Vita S. August.* 2. 4. 5 (PL 32. 108); *C. Acad.* 2. 4 f.

⁴⁹ Cf. 2. 8; *Conf.* 6. 24.

⁵⁰ Cf. *C. Acad.* 2. 8; *De vera rel.* 12; *Epist.* 15. 1; 27. 4.

[51] *Epist.* 27. 4; 32 (Paulinus to Romanianus and Licentius).

[52] CIL 8 *Suppl.* 17226.

[53] 3. 14.

[54] 3. 45.

[55] E.g.: 1. 7, 8; 2. 22, 26; 3. 14-16, 31, 35 f., 41, 43, 45.

[56] See P. Drewniok, *De Augustini contra Academicos libris III* (diss. Breslau 1913). This thesis is vitiated by the assumption that Augustine is incapable of any originality (cf. 66, 68, 70), by one egregious blunder (20 f.), and by a too lively imagination in the noting of verbal correspondence.

[57] Alfaric, *op. cit.* 276, sees very close external correspondence between the two works. His opinion, however, is based on the view that Augustine was using the earlier two-book edition of the *Academica*. Drewniok's thesis, on the other hand, gives much emphasis to the assumption that he was using the later four-book edition. Cf. C. Thiaucourt, 'Les Académiques de Cicéron et le Contra Academicos de saint Augustin,' in *Mélanges Boissier* (Paris 1903) 425 ff. For the general problem of the editions of the *Academica*, see O. Plasberg's edition (Leipzig 1922), and J. S. Reid's (London 1885).

[58] See n. 53 to Book Two.

[59] See n. 29 to Book One.

[60] See n. 55 to Book Two.

[61] See above, n. 16.

[62] Codex Monacensis (11th century); Codex Trecensis (11th century).

[63] *Retract.* 1. 1.

[64] Codex Parisinus (9th century); Codex Remensis (9th century); Codex Harleianus (10th century).

[65] *Retract.* 1. 1; cf. *De Trin.* 15. 12. 21; *Enchir.* 20.

[66] *Epist.* 1. 1.

[67] Cf. 2. 11; 3. 10, 31, and Cicero, *Acad.* 2. 66, 115.

[68] Cf. 2. 11; 3. 18, and Cicero, *Acad.* 1. 40-42; 2. 18, 77.

[69] Cf. 2. 11; 3. 22 f., and Cicero, *Acad.* 2. 91.

[70] Cf. 2. 11; 3. 22 f., and Cicero, *Acad.* 1. 45; 2. 28, 59 f., 66, *passim.*

[71] Cf. 2. 11; 3. 22-32, and Cicero, *Acad.* 1. 45; 2. 59, 66, *passim.*

[72] Cf. 2. 12; 3. 33-36, and Cicero, *Acad.* 2. 24 f., 33 ff.

[73] 3. 43: *Hoc mihi de Academicis interim probabiliter, ut potui,*

persuasi. Quod si falsum est, nihil ad me, cui satis est iam non arbitrari non posse ab homine inveniri veritatem. Quisquis autem putat hoc sensisse Academicos, ipsum Ciceronem audiat. Ait enim illis morem fuisse occultandi sententiam suam nec eam cuiquam, nisi qui secum ad senectutem usque vixissent, aperire consuesse. Quae sit autem ista, deus viderit; eam tamen arbitror Platonis fuisse. The quotation from Cicero is *Academica* frg. 21 (Müller). There is nothing in Cicero's extant works that would support Augustine's view (offered, as should be noticed, with little assurance). Some passages do come fairly close—e.g.: *Acad.* 2. 60, 98; *De fin.* 2. 2; cf. *De fato* 4; *De off.* 2. 8; *De orat.* 1. 84; 3. 67, 80; *Tusc.* 1. 8; 2. 9—but not close enough. Moreover, the quotation given by Augustine does not cover the theory to which he attaches it. It merely states: (1) that the Academics were accustomed to conceal their own view, and, (2) that they revealed it only to those who lived with them up to old age. It does not authorize the statements that that secret doctrine (1) was Plato's, and (2) that they deliberately taught an assumed negative one. If Cicero had in fact expounded such an opinion, Augustine would have quoted him explicitly to that effect. Of course, the whole tenor of Cicero's writings is against Augustine in this, as he himself knows; cf. *C. Acad.* 2. 29 f.; 3. 41; also the notes to 3. 43.

[74] Neo-Platonism was a synthesis of Platonic, Pythagorean, Aristotelian, and Stoic elements, and was the dominant philosophy of the third century A.D. down to the time of Justinian (sixth century). The outstanding Neo-Platonists were Plotinus (the greatest), Porphyry, and Iamblichus. Their doctrine was a spiritual one, bordering on, if not actually being, pantheism. Cf. T. Whittaker, *The Neoplatonists* (2nd ed. Cambridge 1918); E. R. Dodds, 'Neoplatonism,' OCD 602.

[75] *Rev. d. deux mondes* 85 (Jan. 1888) 43-69; cf. G. Boissier, *La fin du paganisme* (3rd ed. Paris 1898) 291-325. A. Naville, *Saint Augustin, Etude sur le développement de sa pensée jusqu'à l'époque de son ordination* (Geneva 1872), had already said something on the matter.

[76] In *Augustins Confessionen* (2nd ed. Giessen 1895) 17. He modified his views considerably, however, in *Augustin, Reflexionen und Maximen* (Tübingen 1922) xvii.

[77] S. Loofs, 'Augustinus,' *Realenc. f. prot. Theol. u. Kirche* 2 (3rd ed. Leipzig 1897) 266 ff.

[78] L. Gourdon, *Essai sur la conversion de saint Augustin* (Geneva 1900).

[79] *Op. cit.* 51; cf. also 45.

[80] *Ibid.* 87.

[81] W. Thimme, *Augustins geistige Entwicklung in den ersten Jahren nach seiner Bekehrung (386-391)* (Berlin 1908) 11.

[82] Intro. viii. Augustine *does* refer to his impending baptism in *De ord.* 2. 27.

[83] 399.

[84] 515.

[85] 527; cf. also 361, 381 f., 393, 398, 518, 525.

[86] Alfaric, *ibid.* 400, 406.

[87] F. Wörter, *Die Geistesentwicklung des hl. Aurelius Augustinus* (Paderborn 1892).

[88] J. Martin, 'St. Augustin à Cassiciacum, veille et lendemain de sa conversion,' *Ann. de philos. chrét.*, nouv. sér. 39 (1898) 307 ff.

[89] E. Portalié, 'Augustin,' DTC 1. 2 (1903) 2273 f.

[90] J. Mausbach, *Die Ethik des hl. Augustinus* (2nd ed. Freiburg i. Br. 1929) 1. 6-16; 2. 390-400.

[91] W. Montgomery, *St. Augustine, Aspects of his Life and Thought* (London 1914) 2. 32-66.

[92] A. Hatzfeld, *Saint Augustine* (English tr. London 1898) 58 f.

[93] T. Bret, *La conversion de saint Augustin* (Geneva 1900).

[94] Cf. E. Gilson, *Introduction a l' étude de saint Augustin* (Paris 1929) 313: 'Dans l'ensemble ce travail est le plus pondéré et, à notre sens, le plus juste que l'on ait consacré à cette délicate question.'

[95] J. Nörregaard, *Augustins Bekehrung* (tr. from the Danish by A. Spelmeyer, Tübingen 1923) 15 n. 2.

[96] Boyer, *op. cit.* 203.

[97] In particular, the preface to Book Two.

[98] See nn. 17, 21, 22, 23, 26 to Book Two, and J. J. O'Meara, 'Neo-Platonism in the Conversion of Saint Augustine,' *Dominican Studies* 3 (1950) 331-43.

[99] See 3. 43.

[100] See 3. 43 and n. 66 to Book Three.

[101] See 3. 43.

[102] A.D. 204/5-269/70. Plotinus was born, according to Eunapius and Suidas, at Lycopolis in Egypt, and lived at Rome until his death which took place in Campania. He taught philosophy and had

many followers, the most notable of whom were Porphyry and Amelius. Towards the end of his life he circulated among his pupils some essays in which he treated of his philosophical system. These were edited by Porphyry in six books with nine essays to each book (hence the name *Enneads*). It is possible that another pupil, Eustochius, also edited independently his own set of notes. Plotinus' doctrine is at once systematic, rational, and at the same time highly mystical. Cf. E. R. Dodds, 'Plotinus,' OCD 705 f.; E. Bréhier, *La philosophie de Plotin* (Paris 1928). There is clear evidence that Augustine had read some of Plotinus' work in translation, and possibly also in the original Greek, in 386; cf. *Conf.* 7. 13; 8. 3; *C. Acad.* 3. 41; *De b. vita* 4; *Solil.* 1. 9; *Epist.* 6. 1. On the question of Augustine's knowledge of Greek, cf. Courcelle, *op. cit.* 137-53, 182, 194. His general conclusion (194) is that Augustine was just barely able to check translations from the Greek by controlling them from the Greek text. It was not until the end of his life that he was able to read and translate Greek with any ease. B. Altaner, however, in one of his most recent studies on the question, 'Die Benützung von original griechischen Vätertexten durch Augustinus,' *Zeitschr. f. Rel.-u. Geistesgesch.* (1948) 77 n. 20, disagreeing with Courcelle, suggests that Augustine seriously occupied himself with Greek well before the year 415. In the present study it is concluded that by 386 Augustine had read at least some sections of the *Enneads*: e.g.: 1. 6; 3. 2; 4. 3; 5. 1; whether in Greek or not, we cannot say. See nn. 11, 14, 15 to Book One; nn. 8, 26 to Book Two; and nn. 3, 61 to Book Three.

[103] A.D. 232/3ʹ - *ca.* 305. He was born at Tyre, studied under Longinus at Athens, and became the faithful follower and disciple of Plotinus, whose biography he wrote and whose works he edited about 300. He was, himself, a prolific writer, regarding it as his mission to popularize the doctrine of his master. The works of his most relevant to our present study are the Περὶ τῆς ἐκ λογίων φιλοσοφίας, Πρὸς Ἀνεβώ, Περὶ τοῦ μίαν εἶναι τὴν Πλάτωνος καὶ Ἀριστοτέλους αἵρεσιν, and, above all, the *De regressu animae*. These works were well known to Augustine in later life, and the case is made here (see nn. 32, 34, 49 to Book One; nn. 10, 17, 24, 26, 29, 63 to Book Two; and nn. 10, 11, 61 to Book Three) that they were probably known to him in 386 and may have had decisive influence on him. It should be noted that Porphyry received more extensive notice from Augustine than any other Neo-Platonist (cf. *De civ. Dei* 10 [all];

162   Notes

11. 2; 12. 21, 26; 13. 19; 19. 23; 20. 24; 22. 3, 12, 25-28), and is also more highly praised than any other (cf. *De civ. Dei* 19. 22; 20. 24; 22. 3), and in particular as against Plotinus, who is always commended as being an interpreter of Plato, and not (as Porphyry!) as an original philosopher (cf. *C. Acad.* 3. 41; *De civ. Dei* 9. 10; 10. 2). We must not allow our present day persuasion as to the relative merits of Porphyry and Plotinus to distort our vision of the position as it presented itself to Augustine. As Courcelle says, *op. cit.* 114: 'la philosophie porphyrienne . . . la philosophie régnante'; 394: 'une seule philosophie subsiste, la néo-platonicienne; le maître des esprits est Porphyre'; cf. *ibid.* 33 f.; 61-65; 394-96. One work of Porphyry's made its author especially infamous among Christians, his Κατὰ Χριστιανῶν, a work which Augustine might have known before his baptism (Courcelle's arguments to the contrary, *op. cit.* 165, 169, 175, 395, are singularly unconvincing). For Porphyry's life and works, see J. Bidez, *Vie de Porphyre, le philosophe néoplatonicien* (Ghent-Leipzig 1913); E. R. Dodds, 'Porphyry,' OCD 719 f.

[104] *Op. cit.* 375.

[105] In: Schriften der Königsberger Gel. Ges. 10. 1 (Halle).

[106] *Op. cit.* 2, 4 f.

[107] P. Henry, *Plotin et l'Occident: Firmicus Maternus, Marius Victorinus, saint Augustin et Macrobe,* Spic. sacr. Lov. 15 (Louvain 1934); cf. the same, 'Augustine and Plotinus,' *Jour. of Theol. Stud.* 38 (1937) 1-23. Courcelle, *op. cit.* 160 f., also criticizes Theiler's thesis.

[108] *Plotin et l'Occident* 94; 'Augustine and Plotinus' 8.

[109] See nn. 11, 14, 15 to Book One; nn. 8, 26 to Book Two; and nn. 3, 61 to Book Three.

[110] See nn. 32, 34, 49 to Book One; nn. 10, 17, 24, 26, 29, 63 to Book Two; and nn. 10, 11, 61 to Book Three.

[111] See n. 158.

[112] D. Ohlmann, *De sancti Augustini dialogis in Cassiciaco scriptis* (diss. Strasbourg 1897).

[113] J. H. Van Haeringen, *De Augustini ante baptismum rusticantis operibus* (diss. Amsterdam: Groningen 1917).

[114] R. Hirzel, *Der Dialog* (Leipzig 1895) 2. 376-80.

[115] Cf. A. Gudeman, 'Sind die Dialoge Augustins historisch?' in *Silvae Monacenses* (Munich 1926) 16-27; also the article of the same title by R. Philippson, *Rhein. Mus.* 80 (1931) 144-50.

[116] Cf. Alfaric, *op. cit.* 400 n. 1.

[117] Cf. Ohlmann, *op. cit.* 79.

[118] *Retract.* 1. 2.

[119] He appeals also to *Conf.* 9. 7, but admits that this text is not decisive.

[120] C. Bindemann, *Der hl. Augustinus* (Berlin 1844) 1. 294.

[121] Ohlmann, *op. cit.* 13 ff.

[122] *Ibid.* 14, 79. To prove that the dialogues are not successful when judged by traditional models, is not, in any case, to prove that they are historical.

[123] *Ibid.* 16, 17: *ex eo quod dialogi hi ficti sunt, illos fictos non esse pro certo concludam.*

[124] *Ibid.* 27.

[125] L. S. le Nain Tillemont, *Mémoires pour servir à l'histoire ecclésiastique des six premiers siècles* 13 (Paris 1702) 88 f.

[126] CSEL 63. 2 n. 1. He fails to notice Van Haeringen's work.

[127] *Op. cit.* 36.

[128] Op. cit. n. 5 (p. 960). Cf. also Boyer, *Christianisme et Néo-Platonisme dans la formation de saint Augustin,* 9 n. 4.

[129] Cf. *op. cit.* 15-24.

[130] He appeals (unnecessarily—cf. *C. Acad.* 1. 4) to T. Dokkum, *De constructionis analyticae vice accusativi cum infinitivo fungentis usu apud Augustinum* (Sneek 1900) to 'prove' this.

[131] *Loc. cit.*

[132] *Op. cit.* 79.

[133] P. de Labriolle, in the introduction to his edition of the *Confessions* (Paris 1925) xv-xvi, and Boyer, *op. cit.* 16 f., rightly insist upon this point.

[134] See below, n. 166.

[135] *Retract.* 1. 2.

[136] Augustine refers (*Epist.* 162. 2) to his *De lib. arb.* as *quae te* (his addressee) *conferente mecum ac sermocinante conscripsi.* It is clear from the context and the book itself that this phrase is used merely to indicate that the work in question is in dialogue form. Ohlmann, *op. cit.* 16 f., rightly regards the *De lib. arb.* as fictional—although Van Haeringen, *op. cit.* 10, denies this. The phrase *libri disputati cum praesentibus et cum ipso me solo* of *Conf.* 9. 7 is an even clearer instance of reference to a literary form. And so also is the term *disputatio* as used here.

[137] Cf. *Retract*. 1. 9 as against Ohlmann, *op. cit.* 16.

[138] See Intro. 5 A.

[139] Cf. 3. 15.

[140] Cf. the prologue.

[141] Ohlmann encounters two of them, *op. cit.* 19 f. In his efforts to solve them he makes assumptions that are purely gratuitous. Other difficulties against Ohlmann's scheme are discussed by Van Haeringen in the course of his own work. They are concerned with the part of Monnica in the debates, the changing attitude towards philosophy of Licentius, and the sequence implied by the beginning of *De ord.* 2.

[142] He is aware of some of them himself, and seeks to explain them away—but quite unsuccessfully. Cf. *op. cit.* 37, 44. He, too, has to make gratuitous assumptions. A further difficulty, not indicated by Van Haeringen, is that in his sequence Licentius, although he forswears allegiance to the Academy in *C. Acad.* 2. 27, and *De ord.* 1. 10, is represented in *De b. vita* 14 (a later disputation according to Van Haeringen's sequence) as being still an Academic. This involves Van Haeringen in the same trouble as beset Ohlmann. It is to be noted that *all* the indications of sequence within the dialogues are equally guaranteed by the record of the *notarius*—a poor guarantee in a dialogue!

[143] By the time Augustine came to write his dialogues, there had not only been many models which he could follow, but these models had been discussed, the dialogue defined, and various types classified; cf. the introduction to Plato's dialogues by Albinus (2nd cent. A. D.), Εἰσαγωγὴ εἰς τοὺς Πλάτωνος διαλόγους (ed. C. F. Hermann, *Platon* 6. 147, Leipzig 1892).

[144] Augustine always refers to them as his own works; cf. *Epist.* 1, *Conf.* 9. 7, *De Trin.* 15. 21, *Enchir.* 7, *Retract.* 1. 1, 2, 3. They were his συγγράμματα, not his ὑπομνήματα (cf. W. Bousset, *Jüdisch-christlicher Schulbetrieb* [Göttingen 1915] 4 f., and A. J. Festugière, 'Le "logos" hermétique d'enseignement,' REG 55 [1942] 96).

[145] Cf. *De ord.* 1. 14, 30, 31; 2. 17; *Solil.* 2. 28.

[146] Cf. *De ord.* 1. 31.

[147] Cf. J. Guitton, *Le temps et l' éternité chez Plotin et saint Augustin* (Paris 1933) xi. 'Ces genres ne sont pas d'ailleurs un habillement; déjà ils imposent à l'esprit certains tours et certains plis. . . . En choisissant un genre, on a déjà reconnu ses maîtres: on se rattache à une tradition . . ., on accepte une compagnie.'

[148] This is said to be an Aristotelian feature; cf. Cicero, *Ad Att.* 4. 16. 2; also Proclus, *In Parm.* 1. 659 (Cousin).

[149] There are some small correspondences between the introductory letters of the *Dialogues of Cassiciacum* and Plato's famous seventh epistle. In both there is autobiography by way of an *apologia;* the intervention of Providence is noted (*Epist.* 7. 326e: *C. Acad.* 1. 1; 2. 1; *De b. vita* 1); and it is asserted that philosophy does not reveal herself except to those who dedicate themselves to her entirely (340c, d, e; 341a : *C. Acad.* 1. 1; 2. 8).

[150] The protreptic was an exhortation to philosophy. See P. Wendland, *Anaximenes von Lampsakos* (Berlin 1905) 81 ff. Antisthenes, Aristotle, Epicurus, Cleanthes, Posidonius, Clement of Alexandria, among many others were authors of such invitations to philosophy. Cf. A. J. Festugière, *La révélation d' Hermes Trismégiste* (Paris 1944) 1. 324 ff., and A. D. Nock and Festugière, CH 14. 1; 16. 1; *Asclepius* 1, for examples of such protreptic introductory letters. Cf. Festugière, 'Le "logos," ' REG 55 (1942) 77 f., for an analysis of a typical instance. Festugière's remark (*ibid.* 78): 'Certes, rien n'est plus commun à l' époque hellénistique que la courte homélie morale adressée à un ou plusieurs auditeurs et que les manuels nomment *diatribe,*' reminds us forcibly that Augustine was following closely a well-established literary *genre.* The instances cited above may well have been known to Augustine. Cf. Nock and Festugière, *op. cit.* 259, 264 ff., 277, 279 f. There was, of course, one protreptic whose influence upon the *C. Acad.* we can immediately trace: the famous *Hortensius* of Cicero, which had made such an impression on Augustine (cf. *Conf.* 3. 7 f.; 6. 18; 8. 17). This book was being used by him in the autumn of 386 in his efforts to make his young friends and pupils interested in philosophy (cf. *C. Acad.* 1. 4). It is not surprising, then, that fragments of the *Hortensius* have been recovered from the *C. Acad.* Similarly, the *C. Acad.* contains echoes of the lost Προτρεπτικός of Aristotle, on which the *Hortensius* was based; cf. R. Walzer, *Aristotelis dialogorum fragmenta* (Florence 1934).

[151] Cf. Plato's *Charmides, Euthydemus, Lysis, Phaedo, Philebus* (cf. Festugière, 'Le "logos" ' 90-92), and *Theaetetus* (cf. 168e and *C. Acad.* 2. 22: in Plato's dialogue Socrates plays the role adopted by Augustine in the *C. Acad.,* Theaetetus that by Licentius, and other disciples that by Trygetius). Cf. Cicero's *De finibus* and *De oratore.*

[152] Cf. *C. Acad.* 1. 11, 16, 24 f.; 2. 10, 25, 29, and Cicero, *De am.* 3. 5.

[153] Cf. *C. Acad.* 1. 15, 25; 2. 30; 3. 14.

[154] Cf. *C. Acad.* 2. 10, and Plato, *Timaeus* 17b. For a proceeding somewhat similar, cf. *C. Acad.* 1. 4, 25; Nock and Festugière, CH 14. 1; Festugière, 'Le "logos" ' 94.

[155] Cf. *C. Acad.* 2. 10-14, 17, 22, 24 f., 29; 3. 4; *De b. vita* 16; *De ord.* 1. 5; 2. 7.

[156] Cf. *C. Acad.* 1. 6, 16; Plato, *Protagoras* 338a, *Symposium* 175e; Tacitus, *Dial.* 4.

[157] Cf. *De ord.* 1. 16, 17, 19.

[158] Cf. *C. Acad.* 1. 4, 15; 2. 17, 22, 29; 3. 15, 44; *De b. vita* 15, 18; *De ord.* 1. 5, 14, 20, 26 f., 29 ff., 33; 2. 17, 21. Both Ohlmann and Van Haeringen fail to take account of *all* the items on this list. Some instances of such guarantees in previous non-historical dialogues are: Plato, *Euthydemus* 272d, 275b; *Phaedo* 59c, d; *Phaedrus,* 228a-c, 230e, 234d, 236e, 242d, 243c, 262d, 263e; *Menexenus* 236b, c, 246c, 249; *Symposium* 173e, 174a; *Timaeus* 20e; *Theaetetus* 143a-c; Cicero, *Tusc.* 2. 9; Macrobius, *Sat.* 1. 1. 5, 6; 1. 6 13; Sulpicius Severus, *Dial.* 3. 17. Hirzel, *op. cit.* 2. 376-80, notes the second-century Gnostic text, *Pistis Sophia,* as making a claim very like that made in the *Dialogues of Cassiciacum.* But the nearest instances we have noted are: (1) Plato's (?) *Epinomis* 980c, d (cf. Festugière, 'Le "logos" ' 93 and 96 n. 5, and Liddell & Scott, new ed. [1940] *s.v.* ὑπόμνημα. The record-taking of the *C. Acad.* is not less likely to be a fiction than the note-taking of the *Epinomis,* especially in view of the prevalence of record-taking in the fourth century A.D.); and (2) Thessalos' record of the revelation granted to him (a document of the first century A. D.—cf. Festugière, 'L'expérience religieuse du médecin Thessalos,' *Rev. Bibl.* 48 [1939] 45 ff.). Thessalos provided himself with paper and ink to take down the revelation as it occurred! A. D. Nock, *Conversion* (Oxford 1933) 289, cites the case of Lucius as found in Apuleius, *Met.* 6. 25 ff.—an instance which, in view of Augustine's schooling at Madauros, the home of Apuleius, may well have been known to Augustine and have given him yet another impulse to employ the idea. There is nothing unusual, then, in the claims of faithful reporting made by Augustine in the *Dialogues of Cassiciacum.* But even if there were, his fiction would be but plausible.

[159] Cf. Augustine, *De b. vita* 6, and Plato, *Gorgias* 447a; *Repub-*

lic 327 ff.; Porphyry, *Vita Plot.* 2. 15 (Porphyry wrote a poem, 'Ὁ ἱερὸς γάμος, no. 74 in Bidez's list, in honour of the anniversary of Plato's birthday); Cicero, *De fin.* 2. 102.

¹⁶⁰ Cf. *De ord.* 1. 8, 10, 11, 13, 16, 17, 19, 20, 21, 28; 2. 12, 17; and, referring to Socrates, Plato, *Cratylus* 396d, e; *Phaedrus* 235d, 236c, 238c, d, 244, 262d, 265a, b; and, referring to poets, *Apology* 22a, b; *Euthydemus* 280a; *Hipp. Min.* 365; *Ion* 542a; *Laws* 888e; *Lysis* 214, 215; *Phaedrus* 260a, *Protagoras* 347e; *Theaetetus* 152b.

¹⁶¹ Cf. *C. Acad.* 3. 45, and Cicero, *De fin.* 4. 80; Plato, *Theaetetus* 171c, d.

¹⁶² Cf. *De b. vita* 35, 36, and Plato, *Phaedrus* 279b; Nock and Festugière, CH 1. 30 f.; 13. 13 ff.; *Asclepius* 40 f.

¹⁶³ *C. Acad.* 3. 15; *De ord.* 2. 12-17, 23-52.

¹⁶⁴ Even Plato himself is said to have had difficulty; see the anonymous (papyrus) commentary to Plato's *Theaetetus* in Berliner Klassikertexte 2 (1905) 28; cf. *Sophist.* 217d. For Cicero, see *De fin.* 1. 29; 2. 17.

¹⁶⁵ One should note that the *Dialogues of Cassiciacum* end with as little reference to the addressee as do those of Plato or Cicero.

¹⁶⁶ *Op. cit.* 79. If Augustine invented the mouse incident, then there does not seem to be any reason why he should not also have invented the improbable vigil of Licentius which is connected with the mouse; the improbable all-night discussion of philosophical questions; the improbable knowledge of philosophical problems shown by Licentius—so profound that his companions are made to regard him as being inspired (although till then he had shown but little interest in such matters). It is extremely likely, in fact, that he made up the whole episode.

¹⁶⁷ *Op. cit.* 22. Van Haeringen's attempt to prove that Trygetius surpasses Licentius in erudition is more amusing than convincing— but it also involves a misreading of *De ord.* 2. 7.

¹⁶⁸ There are some small discrepancies which should not arise if the dialogues were actually based on a record; e.g.: *C. Acad.* 1. 6: '*repeto . . .* sententiam meam.' No such *sententia* had been attributed to him. Cf. the inconsistency in the data determining the order of occurrence of the dialogues. See Intro. 5 A.

¹⁶⁹ Cf. the details referred to in *Retract.* 1. 2. See Intro. 5 A.

¹⁷⁰ In the *Confessions* Augustine was under an obligation not to misrepresent facts. It was far otherwise in the dialogues.

¹⁷¹ See nn. 17, 21, 22, 23, 26 to Book Two. At most there is,

naturally, a difference of emphasis due to the nature of the form, the subject-matter, and the time of writing.

[172] P. de Labriolle, in the introduction to his edition of the *Confessions* (Paris 1925) xxv-xxxii; R. Jolivet, in his edition of the *Dialogues of Cassiciacum* (Paris 1939); and P. Henry, *Plotin et l'Occident* (Louvain 1934) 86.

BOOK ONE

[1] For this type of introductory letter, see n. 150 to the Intro.

[2] For the addressee, see the Intro. 2 F.

[3] In the *Retractationes*, composed about 427, Augustine reviews his writings with the intention of correcting impressions which he did not then wish to be given. Regarding the use of the word 'fortune,' he states (1. 1. 2): 'But I regret that in the same three books of mine (*C. Acad.*) I mentioned "fortune" so often. I did not intend, of course, this word to refer to any goddess, but rather to the fortuitous outcome of events for good or evil affecting our own bodies or things external. Whence we use the words *forte* ("by chance"), *forsan* ("perhaps"), *forsitan, fortasse, fortuito,* words about which we need have no scruple. Nevertheless, we should seek the explanation of all this in Divine Providence. Even then I did not neglect to do so, when I said: "Indeed, it may be that what is commonly called 'fortune' is governed by a secret ordinance; and we call 'chance' that element in things for which we can offer no cause or reason." I said this, it is true; yet I regret that I mentioned fortune there in such a way. For I notice that men have a deplorable habit of saying: "It is the will of fortune," when they should say: "It is the will of God."' For the cult of the Latin *Fortuna* and the Greek *Tyche,* see OCD *s. vv.;* cf. Cicero, *Acad.* 1. 29.

[4] Cf. Cicero, *Acad.* 2. 139: 'Revocat virtus vel potius reprendit manu.'

[5] *Retract.* 1. 1. 2: 'When I said in a certain place: "The fact is that, whether because we have deserved it, or because this is necessary by nature, the divine spirit that is united to our mortal bodies can never reach the harbour of wisdom, etc.," I should either have said nothing on these two points—for the sense could have been

complete without them—or it would have been enough to say: "because we deserved it," (a truth apparent from the wretchedness we have inherited from Adam); and I should not have added "or because this is necessary by nature," since the dire necessity of our nature has justly arisen from the evil that went before.' The passage in the text has a Platonic touch, which could have been derived from many sources; cf. for instance, Cicero, *Acad.* 1. 29. The principle laid down by R. Reitzenstein (Bibliothek Warburg, Vorträge 1 [1922-23] 40 n. 13) in the matter of tracing Plotinian influence (and this holds true for all Platonist influence here) on Augustine is important: before assuming influence by Plotinus one should always ask oneself what may be inspired by Cicero. This is to be recommended especially in the case of Augustine's *Contra Academicos*.

⁶ Augustine says that although at this time he had no settled views on the question of the soul (*De b. vita* 5; *Solil.* 1. 7), nevertheless he was deeply interested in the matter (*C. Acad.* 3. 38; *De b. vita* 4; *De ord.* 2. 24, 44, 47; *Solil.* 1. 7; 2. 27, 32). In general, he speaks of the *anima* (soul) as that which with the body makes up the human composite (*C. Acad.* 1. 9; *De ord.* 2. 6, 19); of the *animus* (spirit) as the intellectual, as opposed to the sensitive or vegetative, part of the *anima* (*De ord.* 2. 6); of the *mens* (mind) as a faculty of the *animus* (*Epist.* 3. 4), which is capable of a lower discursive function (*De ord.* 2. 30, 38, 48, 50) called *ratio* (reason), and a higher intuitional function (*De ord.* 2. 17, 19, 41-42; *Epist.* 3. 4; 8. 2) called *intellectus* (intellection). There is, of course, a certain fluidity in the terminology (*C. Acad.* 1. 22; *De b. vita* 8; *De ord.* 2. 5, 6, 7, 38, 41, 48, 50; *Solil.* 2. 33), but never so as to cause any confusion. Gilson, *Introduction a l'étude de saint Augustin* (Paris 1929) 53-54 n. 1, finds a similar scheme for the whole of Augustine's works. Augustine's *animus* may remind one of the Neo-Platonic νοῦς but it is clearly differentiated from it. It is claimed to be of all things the nearest to God (*C. Acad.* 1. 9; *De b. vita.* 4), but is also said to be definitely not of the same substance as God (*De ord.* 2. 46). In this Augustine emphatically, and for us significantly, repudiates what forms a fundamental postulate of Neo-Platonism. He is puzzled as to the origin of the soul (*C. Acad.* 1. 1; *De b. vita* 1; *De ord.* 2. 17, 47), but favours the idea of a pre-existence (*C. Acad.* 1. 9; 2. 22; *De ord.* 2. 31; *Solil.* 2. 31, 35; *Epist.* 7. 2), and is satisfied that the soul is immortal (*Solil.* 2. 3-5, 23, 32).

⁷ The epithet 'divine' used with 'spirit' is not employed in its strict significance. Augustine at this time also speaks, for example, of *divina philosophia* (*Epist.* 2. 1; cf. *De ord.* 2. 46). The divinity of the soul is mentioned not only by Cicero (*De fin.* 2. 40; *De off.* 3. 44; *Tusc.* 1. 65; 5. 38, 70) among many others, who may have meant it in a full sense, but by Ambrose (cf. *De Noe et arca* 92), who certainly did not attach this meaning to it.

⁸ A favourite metaphor in Greek and Roman philosophical and mystical literature: cf. Nock and Festugière, CH 7. 1 and n. 6; Cicero, *Tusc.* 1. 107, 108; *De sen.* 71; Virgil (?), *Catal.* 8.

⁹ Another such expression. It is connected with the famous adage 'know thyself': cf. Nock and Festugière, CH 1. 18 and n. 47; also below, nn. 12 and 22 to Book Two.

¹⁰ Cf. Cicero, *Acad.* 1. 29.

¹¹ Cf. Plotinus 3. 2. 3, 13. Augustine refers later in *De civ. Dei* (10. 14) to this essay of Plotinus. He is also indebted to it in *De ord.* 1. 1, which is contemporary with *C. Acad.* Cf. nn. 14, 15 below; nn. 8 and 26 to Book Two; nn. 3 and 61 to Book Three.

¹² The distinction between popular knowledge for the masses and philosophical knowledge for the few was much stressed in antiquity. Cf. Aristotle, *Eth. Eud.* 1217b, 22, *Pol.* 1278b, 31, *Metaph.* 1076a, 28, *Eth. Nicom.* 1102a, 26. From this naturally arose the idea of a secret doctrine for the few (cf. Plato, *Epist.* 7. 341c), which was widespread in Hellenistic times (cf. Nock and Festugière, CH 13. 22 and n. 62; *Asclepius* 2; Festugière, 'Le "Logos"' 86), and which is fully exploited in an interesting way in the present work. Cf. 2. 29; 3. 38; and n. 61 to Book Three.

¹³ A synthesis of Christianity and Platonism—cf. 3. 43.

¹⁴ *Nam si divina providentia pertenditur usque ad nos, quod minime dubitandum est.* . . . From a comparison of this text with *De ord.* 1. 1: 'aut *divinam providentiam* non *usque* in haec ultima et ima *pertendi* . . . utrumque *impium*,' and *De civ. Dei* 10. 14: 'de *providentia* disputat Plotinus Platonicus eamque a summo *deo* . . . *usque ad haec terrena et ima pertingere*,' it is clear that Augustine was acquainted in 386 with Plotinus 3. 2. 13, to which the passage in *De civ. Dei* refers. Cf. also *De ord.* 2. 12 (and 1. 2, 4, 18; 2. 51; *Conf.* 7. 19 ff.) with Plotinus 3. 2. 7, 17. Cf. nn. 11 above and 15 below; nn. 8, 26 to Book Two; and nn. 3, 61 to Book Three.

¹⁵ Cf. Plotinus 1. 6. 7; cf. nn. 11, 14 above; nn. 8, 26 to Book Two; and nn. 3, 61 to Book Three.

[16] That is, his *mens*, 'mind.'

[17] The metaphor of waking from sleep is often used in this connection: cf. *De b. vita.* 35; *Solil.* 1. 2; Plotinus 1. 6. 8, 9; Iamblichus, *Protr.* 2. 56; see also in the Bible: 1 Cor. 15. 34; 1 Thess. 5. 6; 1 Peter 5. 8; etc.

[18] Manicheism. See Intro. 2 A.

[19] Here, too, Augustine was to criticize himself later, *Retract.* 1. 1. 2: 'Again, when I stated in that place that "nothing whatever that is discerned by mortal eyes, *or is the object of any perception,* should be worshipped, but everything such should be contemned," I should have added some words so that it would read: "is the object of any perception *of the mortal body.*" For there is a perception also of the mind. But I was speaking then as those do who maintain that perception can be predicated only of the body, and that only corporeal things can be perceived. Accordingly, wherever I have spoken in this way, there is danger of my words being ambiguous except to those who are accustomed to employ the phrase in question.'

[20] See Intro. 2 A and *ibid.* n. 8.

[21] See Intro. 5 B and *ibid.* n. 158.

[22] Cf. Virgil, *Aen.* 9. 312.

[23] Cf. Cicero, *Hort.* fr. 36 (Müller).

[24] In *Retract.* 1. 1. 2, Augustine again remarks: 'I said further: "What else do you think happiness is, but to live in conformity with that which is best in man?" Now what I meant by "that which is best in man" I explained shortly afterwards: "Who," said I, "would think that anything else is best in man but that part of his spirit whose commands whatever else there is in man must obey? And this part, lest you ask for another definition, can be termed 'mind' or 'reason.'"' This, of course, is true; for, as far as man's nature is concerned, there is nothing better in him than mind and reason. But he who would be happy should not live in conformity with that mind—for then he would live according to man, whereas, in order to arrive at happiness, he ought to live according to God. In order to achieve happiness, our mind should not be content with itself, but should subject itself to God.'

[25] Such an opinion of his has not been given in the text; cf. n. 27 below, and Intro. 5 C.

[26] Cf. Cicero, *Acad.* 2. 127.

[27] We have not been told that he had been made judge; cf. n. 25 above.

[28] The argument is nearly always referred to in the case of the hypothetical 'wise' man. Cf. Cicero, *Acad.* 2. 66 ff.

[29] Carneades: 214/213 - 129/128 B.C. He was born at Cyrene, founded the New Academy, made a famous visit to Rome in 156/155 when he argued so successfully both for and against a problem concerning justice that the Romans were shocked. He resigned from the presidentship of his school in 137/136, and left no writings. He denied the possibility of any certitude whatever, but evolved a theory of probability in action depending upon degree of clarity in perception. Cf. H. v. Arnim, 'Karneades,' RE 10 (1919) 1964-85.

[30] Cicero, *Hort.* fr. 101 (Müller).

[31] Cf. Cicero, *Acad.* 1. 43-46.

[32] *Cum hoc corpus, hoc est, tenebrosum carcerem, dereliquerit:* cf. Plato, *Crat.* 400c; *Gorg.* 493a; *Phaed.* 82e; 114b, c; *Phaedr.* 250c. See nn. 34, 49 below; nn. 10, 17, 24, 26, 29, 63 to Book Two; and nn. 10, 11, 61 to Book Three.

[33] Here again Augustine later found ground for correction—*Retract.* 1. 1. 2: 'Although the word ("omen") was said in a joke and not seriously, nevertheless, I would prefer not to use it. For I do not remember meeting the word "omen" either in our Sacred Scriptures or in the written disputation of any churchman; though the word "abomination" *(abominatio)* which occurs often in Holy Writ is derived from it.' The Benedictine editors note (PL 32. 586): 'Nevertheless we do read the word "omen" in 3 Kings 20. 33. But St. Augustine either did not read it in the version which he was using, or, because the remarks there are attributed to pagans, did not consider that the use of a profane word should be approved of from this instance.'

[34] *Ab omni corporis labe:* cf. n. 32 above.

[35] Cf. Cicero, *Acad.* 1. fr. 16, where error is spoken of in terms of travelling on a road.

[36] Cf. Cicero, *Tusc.* 1. 1: 'Cum omnium artium, quae ad *rectam vivendi viam* pertinerent, ratio et disciplina studio sapientiae, quae philosophia dicitur, contineretur. . . .'

[37] Virgil, *Aen.* 1. 401.

[38] But the New Academy retained the process of defining terms; cf. Cicero, *Acad.* 2. 18.

[39] Cf. Cicero, *Acad.* 2. 36.

[40] This Stoic definition is found, for example, in Cicero, *De off.* 2. 5 (for which see the note by H. A. Holden, *M. Tulli Ciceronis De officiis libri tres* [Cambridge 1899] 276), and *Tusc.* 4. 57; cf. also Seneca, *Epist.* 14. 1. 5.

[41] Possibly the proconsul in Africa in 393; cf. O. Seeck, 'Flaccianus' no. 2, RE 6 (1909) 2431. Augustine at any rate knew the proconsul well; cf. *De civ. Dei* 18. 23.

[42] Cf. Cicero, *Acad.* 2. 27.

[43] *Haruspices.* The word (Latin *hira* (?) = 'gut,' and *specio* = 'I look') was applied to diviners imported from Etruria (Livy, 1. 56 .4 f.). The *Etrusca disciplina* of the haruspices was concerned (cf. Cicero, *De div.* 1. 12; 2. 26) with a) *exta:* the interpretation of peculiarities in vital organs, especially the livers and gall-bladders of sheep; b) *monstra:* interpretation of prodigies, such as unusual births; and c) *fulgura:* interpretation of lightning by frequency, location, and effects. Cf. C. O. Thulin, 'Haruspices,' RE 7 (1912) 2431-68; A. S. Pease, 'Haruspices,' OCD 405 f.

[44] *Augures.* These were the official Roman diviners and formed a body *(collegium)* with as many as sixteen members. The etymology of the word is uncertain. Their business was not to foretell the future, but from the observation of signs, especially as manifested by birds, to tell if the gods approved or disapproved of an action proposed. Cf. G. Wissowa, *Religion und Kultus der Römer* (2nd ed. Munich 1912) 523-34; H. J. Rose, 'Augures,' OCD 120.

[45] From the time of Alexander the Great astrology, which claimed to be able to indicate the effect of celestial bodies on human destinies, and, consequently, foretell the future, spread rapidly throughout the Graeco-Roman world, until in Imperial times it affected everyone, high and low, everywhere. It influenced philosophy, especially Stoicism, and medicine profoundly, and in many ways left its mark on the literature of the time. Cf. F. Boll, *Sternglaube und Sterndeutung* (4th ed. by W. Gundel, Leipzig 1931); F. Cumont, *Les religions orientales dans le paganisme romain* (4th ed. Paris 1929) 151-79; A. J. Festugière, *La révélation d'Hermès Trismégiste* (Paris 1944) 1. 89-186; W. Gundel, the articles 'Astralreligion' and 'Astrologie,' RAC (1943) 810-17-31.

[46] The practitioners of dream divination, called 'oneirocritics,' could refer to a literature of their own, practical dream-books as contained in the extant *Oneirocritica* of Artemidorus of Ephesus

and similar works by Demetrius of Phalerum, Hermippus of Berytus, and others. Closely associated with dream divination is incubation (see ACW 10 [1950] 120 n. 173), a practice in which especially persons afflicted with ill-health slept within the precincts of certain shrines, hoping to receive divinatory dreams from the gods Asclepius (god of health), Serapis, or Isis. Cf. T. Hopfner, 'Mantike,' RE 14 (1930) 1268-76; A. S. Pease, 'Divination,' OCD 292 § 3.

[47] Seers, *vates*, who practise *vaticinatio* ('foretelling,' 'prophecy') act as mouthpieces of divine or demonic powers possessing them. Cf. Pease, *art. cit.* § 4.

[48] *Daemones:* Demons (Gr. δαίμων) in Homeric times seem to have been regarded as manifestations of divine power—whether for good or for evil—rather than as the divinities or gods (who were called θεοί) themselves. But in the writings of Hesiod and regularly from the time of Plato, demons were conceived of as beings intermediate between gods and men. In the Bible the term is used to designate the fallen angels or 'unclean spirits.' Cf. M. P. Nilsson, *Geschichte der griechischen Religion 1* (Munich 1941) 201-206; E. Mangenot, 'Démon,' DTC 4. 1 (1911) 321-409; W. Foerster, 'δαίμων,' TWNT 2 (1935) 1-21. For a study of demons as regarded by an early Christian writer, see the monograph by E. Schneweis, *Angels and Demons according to Lactantius* (SCA 3, Washington 1944).

It is stated here that these 'contemptible' beings live in the air (note also the allusion at the close of the next paragraph): regarding the ancient Christian belief that the demons dwelt in the air and in this medium carried on their evil activity, cf. the observations in ACW 3 (1947) 123 n. 68, and 10 (1950) 112 n. 82.

[49] *Ab omnibus involucris corporis mentem quantum potest, evolvit, et seipsum in semetipsum colligit.* See nn. 9 and 32 above.

[50] Keeping the traditional reading: *quae cum essent dicta, prandium paratum esse annuntiatum est, atque surreximus,* as against Knöll.

BOOK TWO

[1] *Vel calumnia vel pertinacia*—cf. Cicero, *Acad.* 2. 14, 18, 65.

[2] *Congrua illi tempori ratio*—cf. 2. 29; 3. 38; n. 73 to the Intro., and nn. 48, 49, 53, 61 to Book Three.

[3] Cf. Cicero, *Acad.* 2. 46.

[4] Cf. Virgil, *Aen.* 8. 370 ff., 535; 12. 739.

[5] Cf. n. 8 to Book One.

[6] Cf. 1. Cor. 1. 24; cf. *De b. vita* 34; *De quant. an.* 76.

[7] That is, the Christian mysteries: see the previous note; also *De ord.* 2. 27.

[8] Multum me . . . adiuvabis . . . si . . . nitaris . . . nobiscum . . . voluntate atque illa tua naturali *mentis altitudine*, propter quam te quaero, qua singulariter *delector, quam semper admiror,* quae in te . . . nubibus quasi fulmen involvitur. . . . Quis enim . . . tantum . . . *lumine mentis emicuit* (cf. *fulgor virtutis* in the same passage): here there appear to be reminiscences of Plotinus—cf. 1. 6. 5. See nn. 11, 14, 15 to Book One; n. 26 below; and nn. 3, 61 to Book Three.

[9] We know nothing more of this.

[10] *Rursus proiecto totius corporis onere recurret in caelum:* cf. nn. 32, 34, 49 to Book One; 17, 24, 26, 29, 63 below; and nn. 10, 11, 61 to Book Three.

[11] That is, Christ. Cf. 3. 43.

[12] Cf. n. 9 to Book One, and n. 22 below.

[13] *Ad summum ipsum modum perventurum esse.* By *summus modus* he means God the Father; cf. *De b. vita* 34: 'Sed quid putatis esse sapientiam, nisi veritatem? Etiam hoc enim dictum est: "Ego sum Veritas." Veritas autem ut sit, fit per aliquem *summum modum,* a quo procedit, et in quem se perfecta convertit. Ipsi autem *summo modo* nullus alius modus imponitur. . . . Ut igitur veritas modo gignitur, ita modus veritate cognoscitur. . . . Quis est Dei Filius? Dictum est, "Veritas." Quis est qui non habet patrem, quis alius quam summus modus?' *Modus* in this connection has more the idea of 'end' than 'measure,' and corresponds to the Greek τέλος: cf. Forcellini, *Totius lat. lex. s. v.;* Cicero, *Verr.* 2. 2. 118; *De fin.*

1. 2; Aristotle, *Metaph.* 994b. 9; 996a. 26. As τέλος, then, it can be used of the final cause and the Good: cf. Aristotle, *Eth. Nicom.* 1097a. 21—that is, God, or God the Father.

[14] The Holy Spirit is meant: cf. *De b. vita* 35: 'Admonitio autem quaedam, quae nobiscum agit, ut deum recordemur, ut eum quaeramus, . . . de ipso ad nos fonte veritatis emanat. . . . Huius est verum omne quod loquimur, . . . nihilque aliud etiam hoc apparet esse quam Deum.' For *admonitio,* cf. παράκλησις in Acts 13. 15; 1 Cor. 14. 3; 1 Thess. 2. 3; etc.

[15] For Augustine's conception at this time of the relations of faith and reason, see 3. 43, and n. 66 to Book Three.

[16] Cf. *Conf.* 6. 24.

[17] *Cum ecce tibi libri quidam pleni, ut ait Celsinus, bonas res Arabicas ubi exhalarunt in nos, ubi illi flammulae instillarunt pretiosissimi unguenti guttas paucissimas.* . . . Here and in what follows St. Augustine gives the first extant account of his conversion. It will be seen that it corresponds with that given in *Conf.* 7. 13 ff. and 8. 1, 28 f.—an agreement which is important. Cf. J. J. O'Meara, 'Neo-Platonism in the Conversion of Saint Augustine,' *Dominican Studies* 3 (1950) 334-43, and nn. 21, 22, 23, 26 below. *Cum ecce:* cf. *Et ecce* of *Conf.* 8. 29. *Libri quidam:* cf. *quosdam libros (Conf.* 7. 13 and 8. 3). The books were Platonist books: cf. *Conf.* 7. 13, 26; 8. 3. In each of these three references from the *Confessions* Augustine uses the same words: *Platonicorum libros* which by their repetition in such a short space acquire emphasis. He does *not* say *Plotini* libros (see n. 20 below), although he *may* have said so in *De b. vita,* where even if he had said 'Plotini libros,' he might easily have meant Porphyry: cf. P. Henry, *Plotin et l'Occident* (Louvain 1934) 154-63, for such an instance. We may conclude with certainty that the works of Plotinus *exclusively* are not meant. *Libri pleni:* cf. Cicero, *Tusc.* 1. 11. Cf. nn. 24, 26, 29, 63 below and nn. 10, 11, 61 to Book Three.

[18] Possibly Aulus Cornelius Celsus (cf. *Solil.* 1. 21; *De haer. prol.*) who lived under Tiberius and wrote an encyclopedia, the medical part of which survives; cf. L. Schwabe, 'Die *Opiniones philosophorum* des Celsus,' *Hermes* 19 (1884), 385-92, and A. Dyroff, 'Der philosophische Teil der Encyclopädie des Cornelius Celsus,' *Rhein. Mus.* 88 (1939) 7-18. M. Schanz, 'Ueber die Schriften des Cornelius Celsus,' *Rhein. Mus.* 36 (1881) 369-71, and P. Courcelle,

Les lettres grecques en Occident (Paris 1948) 178-81, maintain on the other hand that Celsinus of Castabala, the author of an encyclopedia of philosophy, which may have been translated into Latin, is referred to.

[19] *Bonas res Arabicas: bonae res* is a usual expression for costly things or articles of luxury, a meaning further strengthened here by the addition of *Arabicas:* cf. Plautus, *Pers.* 4. 3. 46; 'Capere urbem in Arabia plenam bonarum rerum.' Cf. A. Otto, *Die Sprichwörter und sprichwörtlichen Redensarten der Römer* (Leipzig 1890) 33 f.

[20] *Paucissimas:* cf. *De b. vita* 4: 'lectis autem (Plotini) *paucissimis* libris,' which refers to the same event. Henry, *op. cit.* 89, regards the reading *Plotini* as certain. It is probable, but not certain. Cf. C. Boyer, *Christianisme et néo-platonisme dans la formation de saint Augustin* (Paris 1920) 80 n. 1.

[21] It is interesting to note the reference to this motive here. See Intro. 2 A, where the question of Augustine's worldly ambitions is emphasized. Cf. also A. J. Festugière, 'Les thèmes du Songe de Scipion,' *Eranos* (Mélanges Rudberg 1946) 376 f. See nn. 22, 23, 25, 26 below for other instances of correspondence between the *Confessions* and the *Contra Academicos*.

[22] *Prorsus totus in me cursim redibam:* see n. 9 to Book One. Cf. *Conf.* 7. 16: 'et inde admonitus *redire ad memetipsum*,' and n. 12 above. On this see also the final note in the volume immediately preceding the present (ACW 11 [1950] 270 n. 7) on Gregory the Great's constant stress on 'return to self,' and self-examination. See n. 21 above.

[23] *Itaque titubans, properans, haesitans arripio apostolum Paulum:* cf. *Conf.* 7. 27: 'Itaque avidissime arripui venerabilem stilum spiritus tui et prae ceteris *Apostolum Paulum*'; 8. 29: '*Itaque concitus redii* in eum locum . . .; ibi enim posueram *codicem Apostoli. . . . Arripui,* aperui et legi. . . . The verbal correspondence between the three accounts is close. See n. 21 above.

[24] *Huic tanto bono:* that is, the teaching of the Platonist books. It is clear from the context that Augustine feared to find something in the Scriptures in conflict with the doctrine of the Platonists that so struck him. Why did he immediately scrutinize St. Paul? The answer may be that he knew that Porphyry had attacked the Christians, and especially St. Paul, in his famous polemic *Against the Christians*. Augustine certainly knew this work some years

later (cf. *De cons. Evang.* 1. 23, 24 (A. D. 399), *Epist.* 75. 6; 82. 22; *De civ. Dei* 19. 23) and could have known it in 386. A. Dyroff's view, 'Zum Prolog des Johannes Evangeliums,' *Pisciculi* (Festschrift Dölger, Münster 1939) 88 f., that Augustine had read a translation of Porphyry's attack on the Christians, which indicated a correspondence between Neo-Platonism and the prologue of St. John, and had in this way been led to Christianity, may not be as far from the truth as Courcelle thinks (*op. cit.* 165); cf. n. 103 to the Intro. It is more likely, however, that Porphyry's *De regressu animae* or some other books of his may have had this effect. If this is true—and the evidence of the present study points in this direction (see nn. 26, 29, 63 below, and 10, 11, 61 to Book Three)—then the influence of Porphyry on Augustine at this juncture was paramount and decisive.

²⁵ Knöll and Jolivet read *castissime,* 'most uprightly, religiously,' for *cautissime,* 'most carefully'; *Conf.* 8. 29 has *legi in silentio,* and a little earlier: *intentissimus cogitare coepi.*

²⁶ *Tunc vero quantulocumque iam lumine asperso, tanta se mihi philosophiae facies aperuit. . . .* That is, the reading of St. Paul *helped* rather than hindered his understanding of what he had read in the Platonist books. He says the same thing in the *Confessions* 8. 29: 'Statim quippe cum fine huiusce sententiae quasi luce securitatis infusa cordi meo, omnes dubitationis tenebrae diffugerunt'; 7. 21: 'Inveni quidquid illac, (that is, in the Platonist books) verum legeram, hac (that is, in the Scriptures) cum commendatione gratiae tuae dici.'

In going on to explain how the Scriptures helped his understanding of the doctrine which he found in the Platonist books, he lets us see that Porphyry must have been one of the Platonists—if not in fact the Platonist of greatest importance here—whose books he read. For he says (*Conf.* 7. 13 ff.) that the Platonists, even though their language was not always accurate, recognised the Father and the Son, but because of their pride, they would not believe in the Incarnation. They saw the fatherland whither they should travel, but failed to see the way. This became a favourite theme with Augustine, and we have irrefutable evidence from the *City of God* that the Platonist most in his mind when he referred to this theme, was Porphyry. This will be most easily seen by placing the texts from the *Confessions* and the *City of God* side by side:

Conf. 7. 13 ff.	*De civ. Dei* 10. 29.

(13) Ibi (that is, in the Platonist books) legi *non quidem his verbis* (that is, in the words of the Scriptures; cf. 8. 28: 'Et *non quidem his verbis*, sed in hac sententia. . . .') sed hoc idem omnino multis et multiplicibus suaderi rationibus quod *in principio erat Verbum*. . . . (14) Sed quia *Verbum caro factum est* . . . *non ibi legi*. . . . *Cothurno tanquam doctrinae sublimioris elati* non audiunt dicentem: 'Discite a me. . . . Obscuratur insipiens cor eorum; dicentes se esse sapientes stulti fiunt. . . .
(27) Et aliud est de silvestri cacumine *videre patriam pacis* et *iter* ad eam *non invenire*. . . . (26) In quos me . . . voluisti incurrere, ut . . . distinguerem, quid interesset inter . . . *videntes quo eundum sit,* nec *videntes qua,* et *viam ducentem* ad beatificam *patriam* non tantum *cernendam* sed et *habitandam.*

Praedicas (Augustine is addressing Porphyry explicitly) *Patrem et eius filium,* quem vocas paternum *intellectum* seu mentem. . . . Ubi, *etsi verbis indisciplinatis utimini* (cf. 10. 23, and 24: '*noluit* [of Porphyry] *intellegere* Dominum *Christum* esse principium, cuius *incarnatione* purgamur. Eum quippe in ipsa carne *contempsit* . . . ea *superbia* non intellegens . . .;' cf. also 19. 23; 22. 25), *videtis* (of Porphyry and other Platonists) . . . *quo nitendum sit,* sed incarnationem . . . qua salvamur . . . non vultis agnoscere. . . . *Videtis* . . . *patriam in qua manendum* est, sed *viam qua eundum est* non tenetis.

The identity of the theme in general and in detail is unmistakable. Porphyry is expressly, emphatically, repeatedly, and almost solely associated with this topic which recurs alone and in conjunction with other themes again and again throughout Augustine's works: cf. O'Meara, *art. cit.* 334 ff.

In the *City of God* there is an added element which is always associated in Augustine's mind with Porphyry: not only pride prevented him from recognizing the Incarnation, but also his interest in demonology. Note for instance: '. . . a quibus (theurgis) *curiositate deceptus* ista *perniciosa* et insana . . . didicisti' (10. 26), and '. . . eique (utinam) te potius quam . . . *perniciosissimae curiositati* sanandum tutius commisisses' (10. 27; cf. also 31. 32). That Porphyry is thus certainly behind the scenes in the *C. Acad.*, is corroborated not only by an echo of this topic in 3. 13, but also by an examination of 3. 38-42. See nn. 32, 34, 49 to Book One; 10, 17, 24 above; 29, 63 below; and nn. 10, 11, 61 to Book Three.

There are also possible echoes of Plotinus 1. 6. 4, 5 and 7 in this passage. E.g. 'philosophiae facies' and σωψροσύνης πρόσωπον (4), 'amator et sanctus mirans anhelans aestuans advolaret' and θάμβος καὶ ἔκπληξιν ἡδεῖαν καὶ πόθον καὶ ἔρωτα καὶ πτόησιν μεθ' ἡδονῆς, etc. (4, 7), 'erumpere nitens tortuose ac deformiter inter scabra vitiorum' and ἀκόλαστός τε καὶ ἄδικος . . . φρονοῦσα . . . θνητὰ καὶ ταπεινά, σκολιὰ πανταχοῦ (5), 'in veram pulchritudinem' and ἐρᾶν ἀληθῆ ἔρωτα (7), 'eius incognitae fame' and τῷ μὲν μήπω ἰδόντι ὀρέγεσθαι (7), and finally 'eminere' and προφαίνοι (5). See also nn. 11, 14, 15 to Book One; 8 above; and nn. 3, 61 to Book Three.

[27] We know nothing of this adversary. But see the Intro. 2 F.

[28] A fashionable resort near Naples, often mentioned by the classical authors.

[29] Later, in *Retract.* 1. 1. 3, Augustine commented rather severely on this section: 'But in the second book that so-called allegory about Philocalia and Philosophia is wholly inept and silly. I said that they were "sisters, born of the same father." Actually, the so-called *Philocalia* either is concerned only with trifles, and, therefore, can in no way be considered as a sister to Philosophy; or, if the name is to be honoured because, when translated, it means "love of beauty," and the beauty of wisdom is the true and highest beauty, then in things that are immaterial and highest Philocalia is exactly the same as Philosophia, and in no way can they be, so to speak, sisters.' The Greek noun φιλοκαλία in this meaning is not well attested, but is found in Diodorus Siculus 1. 51. The verb φιλοκαλεῖν (= 'to love the beautiful') is found in Thucydides in a famous connection (2. 40), but on the whole it did not have a wide circulation in classical times.

The present passage is to be compared with one from the *Soliloquies* in order to yield further evidence of Augustine's acquaintance with Porphyry at this time:

C. Acad. 2. 7.

Sed illa (Philocalia) *visco* libidinis detracta *caelo suo* et *inclusa cavea* populari viciniam tamen nominis tenuit ad commonendum aucupem, ne illam contemnat. Hanc igitur sine *pinnis sordidatam* et egentem volitans libere soror (Philosophia) saepe agnoscit, sed raro liberat; non enim philocalia ista unde genus ducat agnoscit nisi philosophia. . . . De nullo desperandum est, de talibus autem minime; omnino sunt exempla. Facile *evadit,* facile *revolat* hoc genus avium multis *inclusis* multum *mirantibus.*

Solil. 1. 24.

Penitus esse ista sensibilia fugienda, cavendumque magnopere *dum hoc corpus agimus,* ne quo eorum *visco pennae* nostrae impediantur, quibus integris perfectisque opus est, ut ad illam lucem ab his tenebris *evolemus:* quae se ne ostendere quidem dignatur in hac *cavea inclusis,* nisi tales fuerint ut ista uel effracta vel dissoluta possint in *auras suas evadere.*

Cf. *De vera rel.* 7 (a text which for other reasons we connect with Porphyry. See n. 61 to Book Three): '. . . cum istis *sordibus viscoque revolare.'* Cf. also *De Trin.* 4. 15 (again a Porphyrian text. See n. 61 to Book Three): '. . . qui non possunt ad *evolandum pennas* nutrire virtutum.'

In *Retract.* 1. 4. 3 Augustine makes a remark about this passage from the *Soliloquia* which he might equally well have made about the passage from the *Contra Academicos:* 'Et in eo quod ibi dictum est, *penitus esse ista sensibilia fugienda,* cavendum fuit ne putaremur illam Porphyrii falsi philosophi tenere sententiam, qua dixit, *omne corpus esse fugiendum.'* This remark needs careful interpretation, but it implies this much at least, that Augustine at the time of writing the *Soliloquia* and, therefore, the *Contra Academicos,* knew Porphyry's view separately and precisely, and very probably knew it as Porphyry's (Courcelle, *op. cit.* 167, interprets this remark in our favour—but too much so, and with too little hesitation). The phrase, *omne corpus esse fugiendum,* is attributed over and over again by Augustine to Porphyry: cf. *De civ. Dei,* 10. 29; 12. 27; 13. 19; 22. 12, 26; *Serm.* 241. 7 (five times), 8. See nn. 32, 34 and 49 to Book One; nn. 10, 17, 24, 26, 63 to Book Two; and nn. 10, 11, 61 to Book Three.

[30] A sample of his poetry, 154 hexameters of rather bombastic quality, survives in certain old manuscripts of St. Augustine's letters, under *Epist.* 26; cf. O. Bardenhewer, *Geschichte der altkirchlichen Literatur* 4 (Freiburg i. Br. 1924) 500; ACW 9. 210 f.

[31] Manicheism.

[32] The *De vera religione*, which was either already prepared or projected at this stage, but was not published until 389-390. See Augustine's letter to Romanianus, *Epist.* 15. 1.

[33] We know nothing about this Lucilianus. He is mentioned also in *Epist.* 5 (Nebridius to Augustine) and 10. 1 (Augustine to Nebridius).

[34] Matt. 7. 7.

[35] Nam modus procul dubio divinus est: see n. 13 above.

[36] Note the wordplay '. . . dies ita *serenus* effulserat, ut . . . *serenandis* animis nostris congruere videretur.' Further on in this section we again have more wordplay: '. . . ut *cura* mea mensa *secura* sit.' In § 17, again, we have '. . . ista *fundere* potius quam *effundere*.' Augustine was fond of such wordplay.

[37] Cf. Cicero, *Acad.* 1. 45.

[38] Cf. *ibid.*; also 2. 59, 66.

[39] Zeno of Cyprus (*ca.* 335-*ca.* 263 B. C.) was founder of the Stoic school at Athens, whither he came in 313. Cf. H. von Arnim, *Stoicorum veterum fragmenta* 1 (Leipzig 1921) 3-72; Cicero, *Acad.* 1. 7, 18, 35, 42, 44; 2. 16, 66, 71, 76 ff., 113, 126, 129 ff. See n. 17 to Book Three.

[40] Cf. Cicero, *Acad.* 1. 40, 41; 2. 18, 34, 40, 77, 83. Such perceptions were called 'irresistible': καταληπτικαὶ φαντασίαι; cf. R. Hirzel, *Untersuchungen zu Ciceros philosophischen Schriften* 2 (Leipzig 1882) 183 ff.

[41] Cf. Cicero, *ibid.* 2. 14, 55, 116 ff., 147.

[42] Cf. *ibid.* 2. 81, 82.

[43] Cf. *ibid.* 2. 47, 48, 51 ff., 88 ff.

[44] Cf. *ibid.* 2. 45, 46, 49, 92, 94, 96, 147.

[45] Cf. *ibid.* 2. 25, 39, 62, 108.

[46] Cf. *ibid.* 2. 32, 99, 100, 110.

[47] Cf. *ibid.* 2. 73.

[48] Cf. *ibid.* 2. 108.

[49] She took no part in the discussions of the *C. Acad.*, but in the *De b. vita* (27) her contribution to the debate is praised by Augustine.

[50] Cf. Cicero, *Acad.* 2. 131. For the view that there was no difference between the New and the Old Academy, cf. *ibid.* 1. 13, 46.

[51] Cf. *ibid.* 1. 16, 44, 46.

[52] Cf. *ibid.* 2. 59.

[53] Arcesilas (Arcesilaus) of Pitane (*ca.* 315-241/40 B. C.) as head of the Academy so vigorously opposed the dogmatic teaching of the Stoics on the grounds that their 'irresistible' impressions (cf. n. 40 above) could be misleading, that he was regarded as founding the New Academy. He left no writings. Cf. Cicero, *Acad.* 1. 44; K. O. Brink, 'Arcesilaus' (1), OCD 79.

[54] Philo (Philon) of Larissa (160/159 - *ca.* 80 B. C.) became head of the Academy in 110/9, and came to Rome in 88 (cf. Cicero, *Brut.* 306), where he had many illustrious hearers, among them Cicero. Cf. Cicero *Acad.* 1. 13; 2. 11, 17, 18, 32, 78; K. O. Brink, 'Philon' (3), OCD 684.

[55] Antiochus of Ascalon (*ca.* 130/120 - *ca.* 68 B. C.) was a pupil of Philo, and later his opponent, and also came to Rome in 88. He was the head of the Academy at Athens in 79-78, where Cicero and Atticus attended his lectures. He insisted in his teaching that the Academic, Peripatetic, and Stoic philosophies were fundamentally one. Cf. Cicero, *Acad.* 1. 7, 16-24, 29, 31 ff., 35; 2. 16 ff., 20, 30, 37, 49, 123, 126, 131 ff.; W. D. Ross, 'Antiochus' (10), OCD 61.

[56] That is, especially Cicero's *Academica;* cf. 3. 45.

[57] This episode may appear somewhat strange to the modern reader. Augustine deliberately introduced the reference to Romanianus. We must believe, then, either that he wished to cause pain to Licentius, or—and this is much more likely, and favouring the view that the *Dialogues* are not historical—he sought some rhetorical effect. Augustine was a rhetorician and is capable of rhetorical flourishes which may have been acceptable in his time, but which now strike us as being bizarre indeed. Of course, one must always keep in mind differences in temperament in different ages and different countries.

[58] Virgil, *Aen.* 11. 424.

[59] Virgil, *Aen.* 4. 173 f., 181 f.

[60] Cf. Cicero, *In Verr. act.* 1. 34 f.

[61] *Satis sit quod cum istis adulescentibus praelusimus, ubi libenter*

nobiscum philosophia quasi iocata est. Cf. the excellent parallel in Plato, *Theaet.* 168e. See n. 151 to the Intro.

⁶² Cf. Cicero, *Acad.* 2. 65.

⁶³ This was later subjected to the following criticism—*Retract.* 1. 1. 3: 'In another place, when I was dealing with the question of the spirit, I spoke of it as "safer in its return to heaven." It would have been safer for me to say "go" instead of "return," because there are those who think that human spirits in punishment for their sins have fallen from, or have been cast out of, heaven and are forced to enter lowly bodies. But I did not hesitate to put it that way, because I used the expression "to Heaven," as much as to say, "to God," who is its author and maker. In the same way the blessed Cyprian did not hesitate to say (*De Dom. Orat.* 16): "For, since we have our body from the earth, and our spirit from Heaven, we ourselves are earth and Heaven." And in the Book of Ecclesiastes it is written (12. 7): "Let the spirit return to God, who gave it." And this must, of course, be understood in such a way as not to come into conflict with the Apostle when he says (Rom. 9. 11) that those who are not yet born have done neither good nor evil. Beyond question, therefore, God Himself is a certain first home of the spirit's happiness. He did not, indeed, generate it from Himself, but neither did He make it from anything else, as, for instance, He made the body from the earth. For, as regards its origin—how it comes about that it is in the body; whether it has its beginning from him who was first created, when man was made into a living soul; or whether in the same way for each individual an individual soul is made—this I did not know then, nor do I know now.'

The expression, *rediturus in caelum,* reminds one of Porphyry's *De regressu animae;* but cf. Cicero, *Tusc.* 1. 24. On the Platonic and the Neo-Platonic doctrine of the pre-existence of the soul, see Augustine's exposition in *De civ. Dei* 12. 26; also 11. 23 and *Epist.* 166 (to Jerome), 17. See nn. 32, 34, 49 to Book One; nn. 10, 17, 24, 26, 29 to Book Two; and nn. 10, 11, 61 to Book Three.

⁶⁴ Virgil, *Aen.* 8. 441.

⁶⁵ *Acutissimis ac doctissimis viris:* cf. 3. 42, *acutissimi et sollertissimi viri,* and *Epist.* 118. 33, *acutissimos et sollertissimos;* see 3. 42 and notes *ad loc.*

⁶⁶ See 2. 29 and 3. 38-42.

⁶⁷ Cf. Cicero, *De fin.* 2. 39; *De leg.* 1. 53; *De orat.* 1. 47; also

Plato, *Phaedo* 91a; *Rep.* 539c; *Soph.* 237b; *Theaet.* 164c - 166b, 167e, 169c.

[68] Cf. Cicero, *Acad.* 2. 60.

[69] Cf. *ibid.* 2. 12.

[70] Cicero, *ibid.* fr. 19 (Müller).

[71] Cf. Cicero, *ibid.* 2. 71.

[72] Cf. *ibid.* 2. 65.

BOOK THREE

[1] See n. 3 to Book One.

[2] Daedalus was a legendary artist and craftsman to whom many inventions were attributed. He is said to have devised two pairs of wings on which he and his son Icarus were to escape imprisonment on Crete by flying to Sicily. The father succeeded, but Icarus perished in the Aegean Sea when he ventured too near the sun and the wax of his wings melted. Cf. Ovid, *Met.* 8. 183-235.

[3] If we compare the text which follows (a) with texts from the *Confessions* (b) and the *City of God* (c), the similarities which may be observed seem to indicate that in all these instances there are reminiscences of a Plotinian passage extracted below. We thus have further testimony that at the time the present work was written—the year 386—Augustine knew something of Plotinus. The passages in Augustine follow:

a) *C. Acad.* 3. 3 (386).

b) *Conf.* 1. 28 (*ca.* 400).

Nam ut sine *navi* vel *quolibet vehiculo* aut omnino, ne vel ipsum *Daedalum* timeam, sine ullis ad hanc rem *accommodatis instrumentis* aut aliqua occultiore potentia Aegeum mare nemo *transmittit,* quamvis nihil aliud quam *pervenire* proponat, quod cum ei evenerit, *illa omnia,* quibus advectus est, paratus sit *abicere* atque contemnere. . . .

Non enim *pedibus* aut spatiis locorum itur abs te (i.e. deo) aut reditur ad te, aut vero filius ille tuus *equos* aut *currus* vel *naves* quaesivit aut avolavit *pinna* visibili aut moto poplite iter egit. . . . *Ibid.* 8. 19: Et non illuc (i.e. ad deum) ibatur *navibus* aut quadrigis aut *pedibus.* . . . Nam non solum ire, verum etiam *pervenire* illuc nihil erat aliud quam velle ire. . . . Cf. also *Enarr. in Ps.* 149. 5.

c) *De civ. Dei* 9. 17 (ca. 415).

Ubi est illud *Plotini*, ubi ait: '*fugiendum est* igitur ad *carissimam patriam*, et *ibi pater*, et ibi omnia'? '*Quae igitur*,' inquit, '*classis, aut fuga?*'

The corresponding passage in Plotinus is found in 1. 6. 8: Φεύγωμεν δὴ φίλην ἐς πατρίδα . . . . Τίς οὖν ἡ φυγή; . . . Πατρὶς δὴ ἡμῖν, ὅθενπερ ἤλθομεν, καὶ πατὴρ ἐκεῖ. Τίς οὖν ὁ στόλος καὶ ἡ φυγή; Οὐ ποσὶ δεῖ διανύσαι . . . . οὐδέ σε δεῖ ἵππων ὄχημα ἤ τι θαλάττιον παρασκευάσαι, ἀλλὰ ταῦτα πάντα ἀφεῖναι δεῖ . . . . See nn. 11, 14, 15 to Book One; 8 and 26 to Book Two; and n. 61 below.

⁴ Quarum rerum in *sapiente* quidam *habitus* inest, earum est in *studioso* sola flagrantia. Augustine had asked what the difference was between the 'sapiens' and the 'philosophus.' In his reply Alypius equates 'studiosus' ('sapientiae') with 'philosophus,' for which see Cicero, *Tusc.* 1. 1. 'Habitus' corresponds to the Greek ἕξις: cf. Cicero, *De inv.* 1. 36; 2. 30.

⁵ Cf. Cicero, *Acad.* 2. 112: 'cum sit enim campus in quo exultare possit oratio'; *Tusc.* 1. 73.

⁶ A mountain in Boeotia, Greece, sacred to the divine inspirers of poetry, Apollo and the Muses. On it were the springs Aganippe and Hippocrene, the latter of which, legend states, sprang forth when the rock was struck by Pegasus' hoof; hence Augustine's reference to Licentius' thirst being slaked by Helicon.

⁷ Virgil, *Ecl.* 3. 104-107.

⁸ Baths were a favourite place for philosophical discussion, so that here Augustine suggests that they should symbolize the proper attitude in which one should hold such discussion.

⁹ Cf. Cicero, *Acad.* 1. 45.

¹⁰ Proteus was a sea-god about whom there are varying accounts. The one most relevant to the present text is to be found in Homer, *Od.* 4. 63 ff., and Virgil, *Georg.* 4. 387 ff. He is a seer, but will not give men the benefit of his gift unless he is forced to do so. When he is captured, he uses the ruse of changing his form into a lion or panther or dragon, or even into fire or water, and thus escapes as his captor, utterly surprised or frightened, relaxes his grip. The secret is to hold him firm through all his transformations until he resumes his natural shape; he is then resigned to give the requested information. Thus, according to Homer, the wandering Menelaus,

having been briefed by Proteus' own daughter, Eidothëe, succeeds in obtaining prophetic advice from the god concerning his home journey. Similarly, following Virgil's account, Apollo's son Aristaeus, prompted by his mother Cyrene, forces Proteus to advise him on the loss of his bees and how to obtain a new stock. For further references to the Protean legend in classical and Christian literature, cf. A. Otto, *Die Sprichwörter und sprichwörtlichen Redensarten der Römer* (Leipzig 1890) 289.

'Investigatoresque eius *numquam* eundem tenuisse *nisi* indice alicuiusmodi numine'; cf. 3. 42: 'animas . . . caecatas . . . *numquam* ista ratio . . . revocaret, *nisi* summus deus. . . .' The parallelism in the words is also found in the meaning. Only a *god* could reveal Proteus and *truth*. The God in question was Christ; cf. 3. 13 and 3. 42. Augustine probably got the idea of the necessity of a Christ from Porphyry; for he says repeatedly in the *City of God* that Porphyry was looking for such a *principium*—the 'mind of the Father'—and had not found it, although he had considered (and rejected) Christ; cf. *De civ. Dei* 10. 23, 24, 28, 29, 32. Proteus occurs again in *De ord.* 2. 43, and also in *De civ. Dei* 10. 10, where Porphyry is very prominent. Cf. nn. 32, 34, 49 to Book One; nn. 10, 17, 24, 26, 29, 63 to Book Two; and nn. 11, 61 below.

[11] This is the same theme as referred to in the previous note and in 3. 42. The phrase further down, 'deceived by false representations,' *falsis imaginibus deceptus*, reminds one of the phrase *curiositate deceptus*, used of Porphyry in *De civ. Dei* 10. 26. Cf. also *De Trin.* 4. 13; 13. 24; *Conf.* 7. 15; *De vera rel.* 7; *De b. vita* 3.

[12] Cf. Cicero, *De am.* 20.

[13] Augustine's lung and throat trouble had been one of the reasons given by him for his resignation from his rhetorical office at Milan: cf. especially *Conf.* 9. 4. On Augustine's state of health and its influence on his thought, cf. B. Legewie, 'Die körperliche Konstitution und die Krankheiten Augustins,' *Miscellanea Agostiniana* 2 (Rome 1931) 5-21; for his weightier reasons—philosophic and religious—for resigning, see C. Boyer, *Christianisme et néoplatonisme dans la formation de saint Augustin* (Paris 1920) 148-51.

[14] Cf. Cicero, *Acad.* 2. 64.

[15] Cf. Cicero, *Acad.* 1. fr. 20 (Müller). J. S. Reid, *M. Tulli Ciceronis Academica* (London 1885) 167 n. 34, refuses to follow Halm in accepting as a quotation from Cicero that part of the fr.

which is given in section 16, on the grounds that 'it has so few genuine traces of Cicero's style.'

[16] The Cilician Chrysippus (*ca.* 280-207/6 B. C.) attended the lectures of the Academic Arcesilas and those of the Stoic Cleanthes, whom he succeeded as head of the Stoic school. He was celebrated for his dialectical acumen and wrote countless works (705 according to Diogenes Laertius!), which were regarded as enshrining orthodox Stoicism. Cf. K. von Fritz, 'Chrysippus,' OCD 188; for Zeno, cf. n. 39 to Book Two.

[17] Epicurus (342/341 - 271/270 B. C.), founder of Epicureanism, was born of Athenian parents, probably in Samos. After learning philosophy in various centres and from various masters, he came to Athens in 306, to found there his own school which was conducted in a garden (κῆπος) that he had bought; hence his school was known as 'the Garden,' just as the school of his great contemporary, Zeno (cf. n. 39 to Book Two), was referred to as 'the Porch' (στοά, hence 'Stoic'), because it was in a porch—a kind of public hall or colonnade—that he held his philosophical discussions: cf. n. 39 to Book Two. Epicurus had a large band of devoted followers, among whom were some women, and led a simple and harmonious life in his community until his death. A few of his many writings are preserved. Epicureanism has traditionally been regarded as an unworthy philosophy inasmuch as it was understood to consider material pleasure as the greatest good, but it has in recent times received a more sympathetic treatment than heretofore. Cf. A. J. Festugière, *Epicure et ses dieux* (Paris 1946).

[18] The Greek cloak or mantle (ἱμάτιον, 'pallium') was the distinctive dress of philosophers. They were often mocked for this by Christian writers; cf., e.g., Tatian, *Or. ad Graec.* 25. 1; Minucius Felix, *Oct.* 38. 6; Augustine, *De civ. Dei* 14. 20. The philosophers also favoured heavy beards—cf. Arnobius, *Adv. nat.* 6. 21, and the passages from both pagan and Christian writers listed *ad loc.* by G. E. McCracken, ACW 8. 599 n. 150. The Cynics (see following note) carried a staff also.

[19] The Cynics (κυνικοί) derived their name either from Antisthenes (*ca.* 455 - *ca.* 360 B. C.) whom some scholars regard as the real founder of the sect, and who taught at the gymnasium Cynosarges outside Athens; or from Diogenes of Sinope (*ca.* 400 - *ca.* 325 B. C.), pupil of Antisthenes and more usually regarded as the founder of Cynicism, who was called 'dog' (κύων: hence, κυνικοί) because he

flouted all convention and cultivated shamelessness. There was no organized Cynic school or doctrine, but, nevertheless, there were very many Cynics in the third century B. C., and later in the East and in Rome from the first to the sixth century A. D. See D. R. Dudley, *A History of Cynicism from Diogenes to the 6th Century A. D.* (London, 1937).

[20] That is, the Academy, a gymnasium in the suburbs of Athens and named from the hero Academus, who was also called by some Hecademus (cf. Diogenes Laertius 3. 9), a name derived from ἑκάς + δῆμος = 'far from the people,' 'stranger'; hence Augustine's allusion.

[21] Cf. Cicero, *Acad.* 2. 112.

[22] Cf. Virgil, *Aen.* 8. 190 ff., where the *semihomo* is Cacus, a fire-breathing, predacious monster, living on the Palatine Hill. When he stole some of the cattle of Geryon, Hercules slew him in his cave.

[23] Democritus of Abdera (*ca.* 460-370 B. C.) is commonly associated with the atomic theory, which, however, he took over from his master, Leucippus. He was wealthy, travelled, and so learned that he was given the name 'Wisdom.' Practically nothing survives of his numerous works. Epicurus incorporated in his own system much of the atomism of Democritus. Cf. A. J. D. Porteous, 'Democritus,' OCD 266 f.

[24] Cf. Cicero, *Acad.* 2. 55.

[25] *Declinare:* this refers to the distinctive contribution of the Epicureans to the atomic theory. Instead of moving in a straight line—as Democritus held—the atoms, according to Epicurus, swerve. This does away with determinism and leaves room for free will. The world itself results from the countless collisions of atoms moving and falling in ever-changing directions. Lucretius (2. 292) calls this swerve *clinamen* (παρέγκλισις). Cf. Cicero, *De fin.* 1. 17-21; *De nat. deor.* 1. 69.

[26] Cf. Cicero, *Acad.* 2. 66, 115.

[27] Augustine now divides the contents of philosophy into physics (cosmology), ethics, and dialectics (logic). The division is traditional: cf. Cicero, *Acad.* 1. 19; 2. 116; *De or.* 1. 68.

[28] Cf. Cicero, *Acad.* 2. 91, 97; *De nat. deor.* 1. 20 f.

[29] Cf. Cicero, *Acad.* 2. 47 f., 51 ff., 88 ff.

[30] Cf. *ibid.* 2. 93.

[31] Refraction, in the case of an oar dipped in water, and the examples adduced in the following—of the changing colours of a

bird's neck and of a tower apparently in motion—were stock objections made by the Sceptics against the dependability of sense perception. Cf. Cicero, *Acad.* 2. 19, 79 (oar and dove's neck), 81; Lucretius 4. 438 f. (oar); Seneca, *Quaest. nat.* 1. 3. 9 (oar), 1. 5. 6 (peacock's neck), 1. 7. 2 (dove's neck). For further passages, cf. J. S. Reid, *op. cit.* 269.

[32] Cf. Cicero, *Acad.* 2. 105.

[33] A minor philosophic school founded by the elder Aristippus of Cyrene (*fl. ca.* 400-365 B. C.), pupil of Socrates. He taught that pleasure of the senses is the highest good and the end of life. His teaching was carried on by his daughter Arete and his grandson Aristippus the Younger.

[34] Cf. Cicero, *Acad.* 2. 45.

[35] Cf. *ibid.* 1. 30-32. The Platonists are referred to.

[36] In *Retract.* 1. 1. 4, Augustine quotes this sentence and remarks: 'It would have been more true if I had said "in God." For the mind enjoys Him as its greatest good, so that it may be happy.'

[37] Cf. Cicero, *Acad.* 2. 51.

[38] Cf. *ibid.* 2. 94 f.

[39] Cf. *ibid.* 2. 71.

[40] That is, a 'Greek' trick, *arte Pelasga*—cf. Virgil, *Aen.* 2. 106, 152.

[41] See in *De b. vita* 3 the picture of the huge mountain of vain ambitions that menaces those who would enter the narrow channel leading to the harbour of philosophy.

[42] *Hortensius* fr. 100 (Müller): cf. *Acad.* 2. 66, 115.

[43] Cf. Cicero, *Acad.* 2. 25, 39, 62, 108.

[44] Cf. *Conf.* 4. 2.

[45] *Samarda(o)cus:* a conjurer, trickster, juggler, charlatan, sharper, vagabond—apparently an African word. It recurs in the *Acta S. Quirini Mart.* 5, and is also found in Greek: see John Chrysostom, *In Epist. ad Ephes. hom.* 17. 3. Cf. Du Cange, in both the Latin and the Greek *Glossarium, s.v.;* also A. Souter, *A Glossary of Later Latin* (Oxford 1949) *s.v.*

[46] Regarding this oath (for the formula, cf. Terence, *Eun.* 331), Augustine expresses his regrets in *Retract.* 1. 1. 4: 'I am sorry also for the statement, "I am prepared to swear by all that is holy." ' The Saint often adverts to the habit of swearing (cf. the note by J. C. Plumpe in ACW 5. 190 n. 137) and states in a sermon (180. 10) that he was very much addicted to it in his youth.

⁴⁷ Cf. Sallust, *In Cat.* 20.

⁴⁸ *Non quid sciam, sed quid existimem;* see Intro. 3, and n. 73 to the Intro. The theory which he is about to advance is referred to by him repeatedly but never with confidence: cf. *C. Acad.* 2. 1, 14, 23, 24, 29, 30; 3. 12, 14, 38, 43; *Epist.* 1. 3: *Illud magis peto diligentius consideres mihique rescribas, utrum approbes quod in extremo tertii libri suspiciosius fortasse quam certius, utilius tamen, ut arbitror, quam incredibilius putavi credendum.* See also *Epist.* 118. 20 (A. D. 410), and *Conf.* 5. 19. There is no relevant evidence in favour of Augustine's view; cf. E. Zeller, *Die Philosophie der Griechen* 3. 1 (4th ed. Leipzig 1903) 508-510; Hirzel, *op. cit.* 3. 216 ff.; V. Brochard, *Les sceptiques grecs* (Paris 1887) 115-8; Van Haeringen, *op. cit.* 100-110; Jolivet, *op. cit.* 213 n. 27; E. Bréhier, *Histoire de la philosophie* (Paris 1927) 1. 348-85. See n. 2 to Book Two and nn. 49, 53, 61 below.

⁴⁹ For this meaning of *consilium,* cf. also *Epist.* 118. 20: *eorum (Platonicorum) quidem consilium,* which J. G. Cunningham (NPNF 1. ser. 1. 445) mistranslates 'nature of their *teaching.*' Similarly, the manuscript reading of *Epist.* 1. 1, *Dei veri artem,* does not need emendation. The providential concealment of their doctrine by the Academics was an *ars Dei;* cf. O'Meara, *art. cit.* 342.

⁵⁰ They formed a religious-political society founded at Croton by Pythagoras (see the following note). It became almost extinct in the second half of the fifth century B. C., but was revived soon afterwards, especially at Tarentum, only to become practically extinct again at the end of the fourth century B. C. This society, which had male and female followers, devoted itself to asceticism and mathematics. A famous Pythagorean was Archytas of Tarentum, known to have been visited by Plato about 387 B. C. See H. Diels, *Fragmente der Vorsokratiker* (5th ed. Berlin 1934) 1. 96-113, 421-39, 440-80.

⁵¹ Pythagoras, son of a cameo cutter, was born about 570 B. C. on the island of Samos. The most learned man of his time, he exerted great influence for many centuries. Besides being an eminent mathematician, astronomer, and reputed discoverer of the theorem named after him, he was a religious reformer, as is evidenced by his founding of a religious sect (see previous note). As a philosopher he differed from his predecessors in that he was not satisfied with explaining the phenomena of nature, but sought to establish from nature, its cosmic order and harmony, norms of human behaviour.

He saw in number a mysterious force that controls the entire cosmos and pervades all the activities of men. He also believed in metempsychosis, regarding the body (σῶμα) as the temporary tomb (σῆμα) of the soul. It is doubtful if he put down anything in writing. Cf. Diels, *op. cit.* 1. 96-113, 440-80; J. Burnet, *Early Greek Philosophy* 1: *Thales to Plato* (London 1914) 80-112, 276-309.

⁵² Pherecydes of Syros (or Syra, one of the Cyclades Islands) was a mythologist and cosmologist who lived in the first half of the sixth century B. C. The ancients regarded him as the earliest writer of Greek prose and the first to compose a work on philosophy. Cf. Diels, *op. cit.* 1. 43-51.

⁵³ ... *pro mysteriis custodita.* It was a widespread fashion in Hellenistic times to attribute secret doctrines to philosophical sects. The idea easily arose from such texts as Plato, *Phaedo* 62b, *Phaedr.* 275d-78c, *Theaet.* 152c-55c, 180bc, *Tim.* 28c (tr. by Cicero: cf. his *Timaeus* fr. 11), *Epist.* 2. 312d, 313c, 314a; 7. 341c, 344c; *Ocellus Lucanus, Text und Kommentar* ed. R. Harder (Berlin 1926) 40 ff. Numenius of Apamea wrote a work entitled, *On the Secret Doctrines in Plato.* Galen states as a matter of course that Plato held two opposing sets of doctrines; cf. 4. 757 (Kühn). The same was said of Aristotle: cf. Galen, *loc. cit.* Something similar was also said of Speusippus (Diog. Laert. 4. 2) and Menedemus (Diog. Laert. 2. 135). Plotinus, Herennius, and Origen are supposed to have made a pact not to reveal the teachings of Ammonius (Porphyry, *Vita Plot.* 3). Clement (*Strom.* 5. 9. 57) and the Gnostics of Alexandria made great use of secret doctrines. When it was brought to the notice of Iamblichus that he was credited with a secret teaching, he said: 'The compliment is gracious, but it is not so' (Eunapius, *Vit. soph.*). Cf. Cicero, *Acad.* 2. 60, and also Nock and Festugière, CH 13. 200, 203 and n. 3, 206, 215 and n. 62, *Asclepius* 297, 341, 357 and n. 10, 390 and n. 289; Festugière, 'Le "Logos" hermétique d'enseignement,' REG (1942) 55, 85 f. See n. 73 to the Intro.; n. 2 to Book Two; and nn. 48, 49 above, and 61 below.

⁵⁴ Polemo (Polemon) of Athens was converted from a dissolute life by Xenocrates whom he succeeded as head of the Academy, which he guided from 314 (313?) to his death in 270 B. C. Cf. Zeller, *op. cit.* 2. 1. 993 f.

⁵⁵ St. Augustine disapproved of this in *Retract.* 1. 1. 4: 'I likewise regret what I said of the Academics, namely, that they knew

the truth, the likeness of which they were wont to call "what-is-like-truth," and also that I said that that "what-is-like-truth," which they approved of, was not true. What I said was wrong for two reasons; first, that I said that that which was in any way like any truth was not true, because this, in its own degree, is indeed true; and second, that I said that they approved of those things that were not true, which things they were wont to call "what-is-like-truth": they actually appproved of nothing and affirmed that the wise man approved of nothing. But since they also called "what-is-like-truth" the "probable," it came about that I spoke thus of them.'

[56] Cf. n. 55 to Book Two.

[57] Cf. n. 17 above.

[58] Cf. n. 54 to Book Two.

[59] Metrodorus of Stratonicea (*ca.* 150-71 B. C.) from being an Epicurean became a follower of Carneades. He so hated all Romans that he entered the service of Mithridates the Great of Pontus. Cf. Diogenes Laertius 10. 9; Cicero, *De orat.* 1. 45, 2. 360, 3. 75; *Tusc.* 1. 59.

[60] A pupil of the great Stoic Panaetius (*ca.* 185-109 B. C.).

[61] In the remainder of this and in the following section Augustine outlines for the first time a master theme which is at once a chief interest of the *C. Acad.* and recurs again and again throughout his works. Parts of this theme have already been mentioned in the *C. Acad.* for example, the concealment of their true teaching by the Academy (see 2. 29; 3. 38) and the necessity for the help of a deity before one can receive truth (3. 11, 13). Here the theme is fully developed. For a complete understanding of all the various parts of this theme and for its full significance as well as for some light on its provenance and personal importance for Augustine, one must examine other instances of its occurrence. The one most closely approximating to the present one is that found in *Epist.* 118. 17-33 (A. D. 410). The passage is too long to quote, but here is a summary:

The pre-Christian Platonists, Augustine writes, knew the truth of a spiritual God, but had not sufficient authority to impose that truth on the masses who were blinded by love of earthly things and enthralled by the flesh. Accordingly, they concealed their own opinions, and contented themselves with arguing against the Epicureans and Stoics. Augustine does not know what their plan was, but he remarks that the controversy between the Platonists and their opponents persisted until the coming of Christ, at whose command the truth which the Platonists feared to publish was immediately believed. There was no such controversy now. The Platonists had changed such of their opinions as Christian teaching condemned, and submitted to Christ in accepting the Incarnation. Augustine mentions especially the school of Plotinus at Rome. In this school were men of great acuteness and ability. But some of them were corrupted by curious inquiries into magic. Others accepted the Incarnation. Therefore the supremacy of authority and light of reason were joined together in Christ and His Church.

If the texts are placed side by side, their mutual relationship becomes evident:

C. Acad. 3. 41-43.

(41) Adeo post illa tempora (sc. Ciceronis) *non longo intervallo omni pervicacia pertinaciaque demortua, os illud Platonis . . . dimotis nubibus erroris* emicuit, maxime in *Plotino.* . . .

(42) Itaque nunc philosophos non fere vidimus nisi aut Cynicos aut Peripateticos aut Platonicos. . . . Quod autem ad eruditionem doctrinamque attinet et mores, . . . quia non defuerunt *acutissimi et sollertissimi* viri, qui docerent disputationibus suis Aristotelem ac Platonem ita sibi concinere . . . *multis quidem saeculis multisque contentionibus,* sed tamen eliquata est . . . una verissimae philosophiae disciplina. Non enim est ista huius mundi philosophia, quam sacra nostra meritissime detestantur, sed *alterius intelligibilis,* cui animas

Epist. 118. 17-33.

(21) Demonstratum errores gentium . . . durasse . . . *usque in tempora Christiana.* . . .

(33) Cum iam Christi nomen . . . crebresceret.

(21) Quos *(errores)* iam certe nostra aetate . . . *obmutuisse* conspicimus.

(33) Emergere coeperant ad proferendum atque aperiendum, *quid Plato sensisset.*

(33) Tunc Plotini schola Romae floruit habuitque condiscipulos multos *acutissimos atque sollertissimos viros.* . . .

(20) Eo rem *successione temporum* esse devolutam. . . .

(19) (Platonici dicebant) id solum vere esse, atque id solum posse percipi, quia *incommuta-*

multiformibus erroris tenebris *caecatas* et *altissimis a corpore sordibus oblitas* numquam ista ratio subtilissima revocaret, nisi summus deus populari quadam clementia *divini intellectus auctoritatem usque ad ipsum corpus humanum declinaret atque submitteret,* cuius non solum praeceptis sed etiam factis excitatae animae redire in semetipsas et respicere patriam, etiam sine disputationum concertatione potuissent.

(43) Hoc mihi de Academicis interim probabiliter, ut potui, persuasi. . . . Ait enim (Cicero) illis morem fuisse *occultandi sententiam suam* nec eam cuiquam, nisi qui secum ad senectutem usque vixissent, aperire consuesse. . . . Mihi ergo certum est nusquam prorsus a Christi *auctoritate* discedere. . . . Quod autem subtilissima *ratione* persequendum est . . . apud Platonicos me interim quod sacris nostris non repugnet reperturum esse confido.

bile et sempiternum est, precipi autem sola intellegentia. . . .

(17) Non valentes illi *auctoritate* turbas terrenarum rerum dilectione *caecatas* ad invisibilium fidem ducere . . . animo . . . *purgato ab omni labe humanarum cupiditatum.* . . .

(20) . . . Platonici . . . neque docerent carni deditos . . . donec ad eum habitum perduceretur animus quo ista capiuntur. . . .

(17, cf. 20) Omnibus enim defuit *divinae humilitatis exemplum* quod . . . per Dominum nostrum Iesum Christum inlustratum est. . . .

(33) Platonici . . . non habentes divinam personam, qua imperarent fidem. . . .

(20, cf. 17) Platonici . . . elegerunt *occultare sententiam suam.*

(33) *Sententiam suam tegere* quaerendam quam polluendam proferre maluerunt. . . . Itaque totum *culmen auctoritatis lumenque rationis* in illo uno salutari nomine (sc. Christi) atque in una eius ecclesia recreando et reformando humano generi constitutum est.

It is manifest that these two texts refer to the same topic. While it is certain that Plotinus is the one Platonist whose name is *mentioned* in *Epist.* 118, it is equally certain that Porphyry is the Platonist *meant* above any other. For the reference is not to *Plotinus* but to his *school* and *disciples*. There can be no hesitation in saying that Porphyry was *the* disciple of Plotinus. It is to be noted that the very same adjectives, *acutissimi et sollertissimi,* are applied to these disciples in *C. Acad.* as well as in *Epist.* 118. Porphyry, then, as in some other places of the *C. Acad.* (see nn. 32, 34, 49 to Book One; nn. 10, 17, 24, 26, 29, 63 to Book Two; and nn. 10, 11 above), is behind the scenes here too. In any case, we have further evidence on this point. When Augustine says in *Epist.* 118. 33 that some of the disciples of Plotinus were corrupted by curious inquiries into magic—*magicarum artium depravati*—we are certain that he is referring mostly to Porphyry. For in *De civ. Dei* 10. 24-32 he explicitly accuses Porphyry, and Porphyry alone, of this (cf. also *De Trin.* 4. 13-15; 13. 24; *De doctr. Christ.* 2. 40; *De vera rel.* 7; *De ord.* 2. 27). Moreover, in *De civ. Dei* 10. 24-32 Augustine deals with the topic outlined in the passage from *C. Acad.* and *Epist.* 118 which we have been comparing, and Porphyry is *the* Platonist emphatically associated with the topic (cf. the association of the *universalis via* with Porphyry: the phrase occurs twenty times in the Porphyrian *De civ. Dei* 10. 32). Finally, the same passages from the *City of God* and *Letter* 118 deal also with the topic (which is part of the present one) outlined in *Conf.* 7. 13 ff., which we have connected with *C. Acad.* 2. 6 (see n. 26 to Book Two) and which also supposes that Porphyry is in question.

From the comparison, then, of texts from the *De civ. Dei, Epist.* 118, *Conf.,* and *C. Acad.* we get a full idea of a view which much occupied Augustine all his life. Its occurrence in the *C. Acad.* is of particular importance and significance, for it at once lets us see how he thought of Neo-Platonism (or Platonism as he called it) vis-à-vis Christianity, and which Platonist played the vital role in his conversion. In brief, the full topic is as follows:

The Platonists believed in the Father and the Son, but were convinced that the mass of men were incapable of receiving this true spiritual doctrine, unless the Son of God came to impose an authoritative way for them. They had not discovered such an authority as yet, and, consequently, in order to save the masses from believing in Stoic materialism, the Platonists taught (in pretence) that no teaching whatever could be trusted, since nothing could be known. Augustine, for his part, and some of the Platonists, had accepted Christ as the Son of God and the way of authority for the masses. Others of the Platonists had refused to believe in Christ, because of His Incarnation and His death on the Cross. Their pride and dealings in demonology had prevented them from seeing the truth. Now, however, the Platonists could teach their real doctrine: for men now knew not only where to go (to their Fatherland), but how to go (through Christ). The synthesis of Christianity and Platonism gave a way that was both one of faith (authority) and reason. The first step on this way, as Augustine had experienced in his own case, was the acceptance of the Incarnation. Through it one grew strong enough to learn the truth. According to Augustine himself, Porphyry had suggested most of these ideas to him.

Apart from the texts already mentioned, this topic is dealt with at great length in *De vera religione* 7 (A. D. 386-390), where some of the objections against Christianity made by Porphyry are discussed (cf. also *De civ. Dei* 10. 32; *Epist.* 75. 6; 82. 22; 102. 8; *De Trin.* 4. 13-15 [A. D. 400-416]; *De quant. an.* 76 [A. D. 388]; *Solil.* 1. 2, 6, 23, 24; *De ord.* 2. 16, 27).

From all this it clearly emerges that Augustine in 386 accepted Christianity without reservation and in opposition to the Neo-Platonist, Porphyry, who had most helped him, perhaps, at this stage. At the same time he looked to Neo-Platonism for help in the understanding of problems (see 3. 43). And, finally, Porphyry played an important, if not actually a vital, part in his conversion. Cf. O'Meara, *art. cit.* 331-43. See n. 73 to the Intro.; n. 2 to Book Two; and nn. 48, 49, 53 above.

⁶² The followers of Aristotle. The Περίπατος was the covered gymnasium or walking place where Aristotle discussed philosophy.

⁶³ Cf. Cicero, *Acad.* 1. 17, 18, 22, 23.

⁶⁴ *Acad.* fr. 21 (Müller).

⁶⁵ Quae sit autem ista, deus viderit; cf. Cicero, *Tusc.* 1. 23: quae vera sit, deus aliqui viderit.

⁶⁶ Cf. *De ord.* 2. 16, 25, 27. Augustine in a number of texts from the time of the *C. Acad.* sets forth his views on the relations, as he then conceived them, between authority and reason. He was very interested—even to excess, as he says (*Epist.* 3. 3; *De ord.* 2. 44, 50; *Solil.* 1. 8)—in the findings of reason. There is sufficient evidence to show that when he was writing the *C. Acad.* he believed: 1) that authority could dispense entirely with reason (cf. *C. Acad.* 3. 11, 13, 42; *De ord.* 2. 16, 26, 27, 46); 2) that authority aided by reason

was more desirable than authority alone (cf. *De ord.* 1. 32; 2. 16, 26); 3) that reason depended on some authority so that it might begin to operate (cf. *De ord.* 2. 26; *Solil.* 1. 12-15); and 4) that reason could arrive at an understanding of everything taught by authority. The last item may cause some surprise, but, nevertheless, it is found in many texts, and especially in the *De libero arbitrio* (388-391/395) 2. 5 f.:

'Quamquam haec inconcussa fide teneam, tamen, *quia cognitione nondum teneo*, ita quaeramus quasi omnia incerta sint. . . . Nisi enim *aliud esset credere*, et *aliud intellegere*, et primo credendum esset, quod magnum et divinum intellegere cuperemus, frustra Propheta dixisset: "Nisi credideritis, non intellegetis." Ipse quoque Dominus noster et dictis et factis ad credendum primo hortatus est, quos ad salutem vocavit. Sed postea cum de ipso dono loqueretur, quod erat daturus credentibus, *non* ait: "Haec est autem vita aeterna *ut credant*," sed, "Haec est," inquit, "vita aeterna *ut cognoscant*. . . ." Deinde iam credentibus dicit: "Quaerite et invenietis"; nam neque inventum dici potest, quod incognitum creditur; neque quisquam inveniendo Deo sit idoneus, nisi ante crediderit quod est *postea* cogniturus. . . .'

Cf. also *C. Acad.* 1. 3; 3. 43; *De ord.* 2. 16; 44: "Eruditi nomine dignissimus *non temere* iam quaerit illa divina non iam credenda solum, verum etiam contemplanda, *intellengenda* atque retinenda'; 50; *Solil.* 1. 8, 12, 15; *Epist.* 3. 3. Augustine believed that there could be no conflict between the true conclusions of reason (which always depended upon God for illumination) and the authority of Christ: both were guaranteed by the same author, God. They were independent, but co-ordinated approaches to the same end. There was no question of subordinating the one to the other. And while the way of faith and authority was infallible and indispensible, that of reason perfected that of authority. It is in the light of these principles that we should judge his attitude towards Christianity and Neo-Platonism. The one was *always* right; the other, *often*. He himself could see that the conclusions of 'reason' and Neo-Platonism were not always the same (see nn. 6 to Book One, and 61 above).

[67] Regarding this and similar passages (2. 24, 3. 37), Augustine remarked in *Retract.* 1. 1. 4: 'Rightly, too, am I displeased with the praise with which I so exalted Plato and the Platonists, or Aca-

demic philosophers, as should never have been done in the case of impious men—especially since Christian doctrine has to be defended against their great errors.'

[68] That is, Cicero's *Academica*.

[69] Again Augustine corrected himself, *Retract*. 1. 1. 4: 'Further, as regards my statement that my own arguments were trifling in comparison with those used by Cicero in his books about the Academics: I, in fact, refuted his arguments with most cogent reasoning; and, though what I said was said by way of a joke and is, of course, ironical, nevertheless I should not have said it.'

INDEX

INDEX

203

ANCIENT CHRISTIAN WRITERS

The Works of the Fathers in Translation

Edited by

J. QUASTEN, S. T. D., and J. C. PLUMPE, Ph. D.